FRANCE

FRANCE

By the Editors of Time-Life Books

TIME-LIFE BOOKS   ○   ALEXANDRIA, VIRGINIA

TIME LIFE BOOKS

Other Publications:

HEALTHY HOME COOKING
UNDERSTANDING COMPUTERS
YOUR HOME
THE ENCHANTED WORLD
THE KODAK LIBRARY OF
  CREATIVE PHOTOGRAPHY
GREAT MEALS IN MINUTES
THE CIVIL WAR
PLANET EARTH
COLLECTOR'S LIBRARY OF THE CIVIL WAR
THE EPIC OF FLIGHT
THE GOOD COOK
WORLD WAR II
HOME REPAIR AND IMPROVEMENT
THE OLD WEST

This volume is one in a series of books describing countries of the world — their natural resources, peoples, histories, economies and governments.

For information on and a full description of any of the Time-Life Books series listed above, please write:
Reader Information
Time-Life Books
541 North Fairbanks Court
Chicago, Illinois 60611

Cover: The 17th Century façade of the Château of Cheverny, in the Loire-et-Cher department south of Paris, dwarfs a small Citroën car parked in front.

Pages 1 and 2: The fasces, shown on page 1, is an emblem used since the Revolution of 1789 to symbolize the French republic. It represents the bundle of rods carried by the lictors — officials of ancient Rome — as a symbol of their authority. France's national flag, the tricolor, is shown on the following page.

Front and back endpapers: A topographic map showing the major rivers, mountain ranges and other natural features of France appears on the front endpaper; the back endpaper shows the country's 22 regions and principal cities.

Time-Life Books Inc.
is a wholly owned subsidiary of

TIME INCORPORATED

FOUNDER: Henry R. Luce 1898-1967

Editor-in-Chief: Henry Anatole Grunwald
President: J. Richard Munro
Chairman of the Board: Ralph P. Davidson
Corporate Editor: Ray Cave
Group Vice President, Books: Reginald K. Brack Jr.
Vice President, Books: George Artandi

TIME-LIFE BOOKS INC.

EUROPEAN EDITOR: Kit van Tulleken
Design Director: Ed Skyner
Photography Director: Pamela Marke
Chief of Research: Vanessa Kramer
Chief Sub-Editor: Ilse Gray

LIBRARY OF NATIONS

Editorial Staff for *France*
Editor: Tony Allan
Researchers: Susie Dawson (principal); Christine Hinze
Designer: Mary Staples
Sub-Editor: Sally Rowland
Picture Coordinator: Peggy Tout
Editorial Assistant: Molly Oates

EDITORIAL PRODUCTION

Chief: Ellen Brush
Traffic Coordinators: Stephanie Lee, Jane Lillicrap
Editorial Department: Theresa John, Debra Lelliott, Sylvia Osborne

Valuable help was given in the preparation of this volume by Maria Vincenza Aloisi and Josephine du Brusle (Paris).

Contributors: The chapter texts were written by John Ardagh, Frederic V. Grunfeld, Stephen Hugh-Jones, Alan Lothian and Russell Miller.

Assistant Editor for the U.S. Edition: Karin Kinney

CONSULTANTS

John Ardagh is the author of two comprehensive surveys of modern France, *The New France* and *France in the 1980s*. A freelance journalist and broadcaster, he works regularly for the British Broadcasting Corporation, the London *Times* and the French news magazine *Le Point.*

Douglas Johnson is Professor of French History at University College, London, and is the author of numerous books on France.

Second printing. Revised 1986.

Printed in U.S.A.
Published simultaneously in Canada.
School and library distribution by Silver Burdett Company, Morristown, New Jersey.

TIME-LIFE is a trademark of Time Incorporated U.S.A.

Library of Congress Cataloguing in Publication Data
Main entry under title:
France.
  (Library of Nations)
  Bibliography: p. 157
  Includes index.
  1. France. I. Time-Life Books. II. Series: Library of Nations (Alexandria, Va.)
DC17.F652 1985   944   85-20531
ISBN 0-8094-5124-7
ISBN 0-8094-5125-5 (lib. bdg.)

CONTENTS

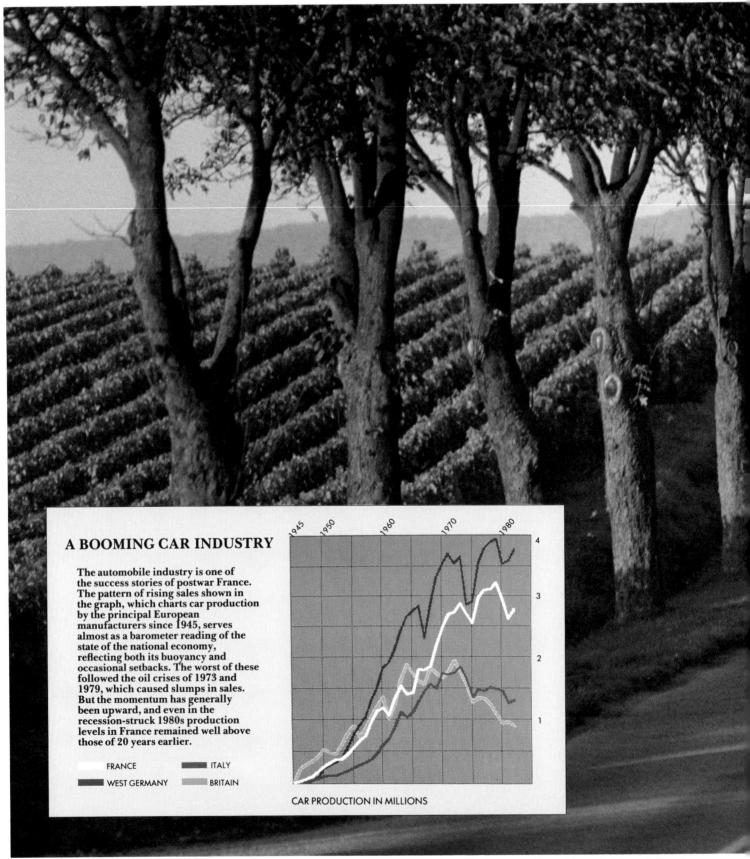

A BOOMING CAR INDUSTRY

The automobile industry is one of
the success stories of postwar France.
The pattern of rising sales shown in
the graph, which charts car production
by the principal European
manufacturers since 1945, serves
almost as a barometer reading of the
state of the national economy,
reflecting both its buoyancy and
occasional setbacks. The worst of these
followed the oil crises of 1973 and
1979, which caused slumps in sales.
But the momentum has generally
been upward, and even in the
recession-struck 1980s production
levels in France remained well above
those of 20 years earlier.

FRANCE   ITALY

WEST GERMANY   BRITAIN

CAR PRODUCTION IN MILLIONS

A Citroën Dyane speeds past vineyards on a tree-lined road near Sancerre in central France. In 1979, the average French household spent almost one

seventh of its budget on cars, and 80 per cent of travel was by automobile.

PATTERNS OF ENERGY CONSUMPTION

With few domestic oil or gas supplies and dwindling stocks of coal, France faces a perennial energy problem. The predicament has become more acute as demand increases, though government efforts since the oil crisis of the early 1970s to reduce consumption have managed to slow the rate of growth.

Faced with limited natural resources, the nation has concentrated on developing hydroelectric and nuclear power. More than 30 dams have been built since World War II and France's hydroelectric potential is exploited almost to the full. But the nuclear contribution is expanding; its share of total energy output is projected to increase from 7 per cent in 1980 to 30 per cent by the year 2000.

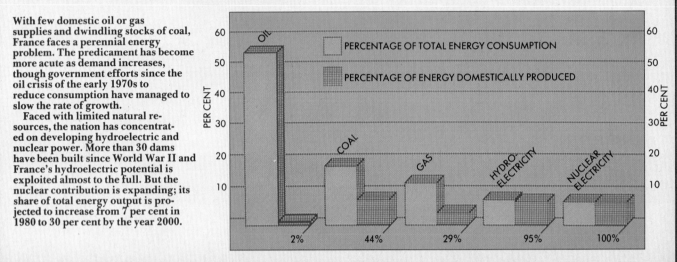

PERCENTAGE OF TOTAL ENERGY CONSUMPTION

PERCENTAGE OF ENERGY DOMESTICALLY PRODUCED

OIL — 2%
COAL — 44%
GAS — 29%
HYDRO-ELECTRICITY — 95%
NUCLEAR ELECTRICITY — 100%

PER CENT

Near Lyon in central France, the cooling towers of the nuclear power plant at Bugey loom through the dusk. Besides producing vital electrical power,

the rapidly expanding nuclear industry provides the country with an export market for its acquired expertise.

A DECLINE IN RELIGIOUS OBSERVANCE

Roman Catholicism is the predominant faith in France, claiming the allegiance of 86 per cent of the population. But the Church and its hierarchy have suffered a sharp loss of influence in postwar years. Church attendance has declined steeply, and a 1979 poll revealed that only 14 per cent of Catholics in France now regularly attend Mass. The Church has even had difficulty in recruiting enough priests to replenish its own ranks: In the early 1980s, only 100 new priests were ordained each year, compared with 1,000 twenty years earlier.

Yet among the minority who are religiously active, there is a fresh vigor. Radical priests have brought a new commitment to confronting social problems, and clergy and laymen have been showing renewed zeal in seeking more direct and personal forms of worship, often through informal prayer sessions and community work. Protestants, who account for only 1.5 per cent of the population, are no longer at loggerheads with the Catholics. Other substantial religious minorities include France's estimated two million Muslims — most of them immigrant workers from North Africa — and some 650,000 Jews.

Outside the sanctuary of Lourdes, France's principal place of pilgrimage, an attendant receives giant candles from the faithful and sets them on stands

to burn as symbols of prayer. Some three million pilgrims, invalids and sightseers visit the town every year.

WIDE-RANGING STATE PATRONAGE FOR THE ARTS

Culture in France has long been regarded as a symbol of national prestige as well as an indicator of the quality of life, and has considerable governmental encouragement. In recent years, the most publicized vehicles for government sponsorship have been the Maisons de la Culture, multipurpose arts centers set up in 15 cities to bring culture to the provinces. However, the centers — used to stage plays, films, concerts, lectures and exhibitions — have been expensive, and the current trend is for smaller units. Paris — still the cultural center of France — has not been left behind; projects of the 1970s and 1980s included the Pompidou Center, and plans to expand and refurbish the Louvre Museum and to build a new opera house.

Festooned with blue air-conditioning ducts and green pipes for electric cables, the Pompidou Center, opened in Paris in 1977, is the most ambitious of

the government-subsidized art centers — and the most successful, with more visitors each day than the Louvre and Eiffel Tower.

13

A NATION OF WINE LOVERS

The French drink more wine than any other people in the world, both in overall quantity and per capita. And, among the top 10 wine-producing countries, France is second only to Italy; together, they make almost half the world's wine. France's share has declined in recent years, however, as comparative newcomers to wine-growing — the U.S.S.R., the U.S. and South Africa — have increased their output. But the high rate of domestic consumption and a tradition of quality, bolstered by a closely supervised grading system and a policy of subsidizing growers who upgrade their vine stock, seem likely to ensure a healthy future for one of France's most celebrated products.

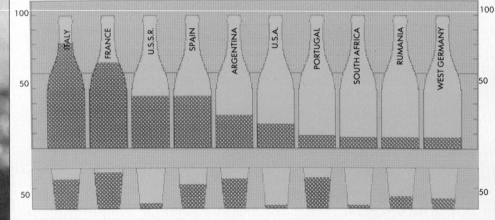

PRODUCTION (100 MILLION LITERS)

ITALY FRANCE U.S.S.R. SPAIN ARGENTINA U.S.A. PORTUGAL SOUTH AFRICA RUMANIA WEST GERMANY

CONSUMPTION PER CAPITA (IN LITERS)

A grape picker harvests a crop of Chardonnay grapes at Cumières, near Épernay in the Champagne region. More than 2.5 million acres of French land

are planted with vines; the greatest concentration is in Languedoc-Roussillon on the western Mediterranean coast.

A BOOM IN PARTICIPATION SPORTS

The increasing affluence and short-ened working hours of postwar France have strongly boosted leisure activities of all kinds, and, in particular, partici-pation in sports. By 1980, six million people belonged to French sports clubs — three times as many as in 1967. Tennis facilities increased three-fold over the same period, and almost 1.5 million amateurs now play soccer. Fishing and horseback riding have both enjoyed phenomenal increases in popularity, and the mountains of France annually attract some four million skiers.

For people going on vacation, the beaches have exercised a growing attraction. In the 20 years from 1958, the number of people choosing to spend their vacations by the sea dou-bled, and private boats and yachts in-creased from around 20,000 to nearly half a million.

The government has played its part in this democratization of leisure. A concerted effort by national and local authorities to improve local facilities has given almost every town a public swimming pool, and various schemes provide subsidized skiing trips and seaside or country vacations for chil-dren of poorer families.

At Autrans, an Alpine ski resort in the Isère Valley, some of the 10,000 competitors in a skiing marathon set off in relays. Once an expensive pastime

for dedicated enthusiasts, skiing has become a mass leisure activity; the national ski federation now has more than half a million members.

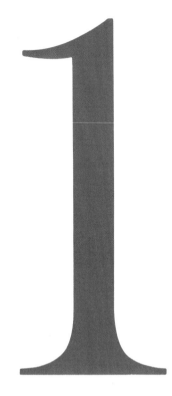

A NATION ON THE MOVE

Summer visitors thronging the Pont d'Iéna in Paris look down on a *bateau-mouche* — one of the sightseeing boats that ply the Seine hourly. Behind, the iron-latticed Eiffel Tower, at 1,056 feet Paris' loftiest edifice, frames the capital's second-highest building, the 693-foot Montparnasse Tower.

"As happy as God in France," goes an old German saying, based less on envy than on admiration and the knowledge that no other country in Europe has been so blessed with natural advantages. By European standards, France is large: At something over 200,000 square miles, it covers more than the combined areas of Britain and West Germany. Partly by reason of its size, but more on account of a geographical position precisely in the center of the northern temperature zone and bridging the Atlantic and the Mediterranean, France has room for every climate and every type of agriculture to be found in Europe. *L'hexagone*, as French writers like to call it, imposing a neat geometry on the battered, six-sided outline of their country, is a kind of continent in miniature, with a cool, oceanic west, an interior, watered by great rivers, whose landscapes range from the Alpine to the near-prairie, and a glorious Mediterranean south.

France has room, too, for her people. At roughly 250 inhabitants per square mile, the population density is less than that of any nation in the European Community other than Greece and Ireland, and the men and women who inhabit France are almost as varied — in their appearance, customs and temperament — as the terrains they live in. Yet despite the physical distance and the differing lifestyles that separate a Norman farmer from a winegrower in Provence, a Breton fisherman from a miner in Lorraine, or a Gascon schoolteacher from a manager in Paris, all are imbued with a sense of nationhood and a cultural identity that since the Middle Ages have fascinated the outside world — and, of course, themselves, for no one is more intrigued by Frenchness than the French.

This is the land of *la France éternelle*, the eternal France, a heady compound of the concrete and the abstract, the real and the imagined. The rich soil, and the sweat and blood of the generations who have worked it; dour peasant hamlets and calm provincial towns; Liberty, Equality, Fraternity; the quiet drinkers in a rural café; grapes ripening on a sun-baked hill; a love of order and a distrust of authority; the bubbling vitality of Paris; a war memorial that is black with names amid a gaunt little village in the mountains. These things are France; the list is endless.

The list is endless because *la France éternelle* does not mean a France that does not change. On the contrary, many more modern images could be added to the roster: the *Autoroute du Soleil*, the Highway of the Sun, in August, piping southward an unending stream of the Renaults and Citroëns of France's recent prosperity, past signposts pointing blandly at historic sites; the high-technology weapons that made France one of the world's largest arms exporters; the pioneering high-speed train flashing between Paris and Lyon at more than 150 miles per hour.

1

Such manifestations of progress may be less evocative than the blue, white and red tricolor that floats impassively above each town and village *mairie*, or town hall, on national holidays, but they are no less French.

Since World War II, France has changed as much as any other Western country and a good deal more than most. In the 1930s, the economy was moribund; the population was shrinking, partly as a result of the loss of 1.4 million young men killed during World War I; the nation was in a state of gloom and defeatism. Paradoxically, the German invasion of 1940 and the trauma of the subsequent years of Occupation injected France with a new determination and purpose. With apparent single-mindedness, France catapulted herself out of the doldrums into a prosperous, technologically advanced society. The phrase "economic miracle" is generally used to describe the German recovery from wartime ruin; yet throughout the 1950s and the 1960s, France's rate of growth generally exceeded that of Germany.

The effects of so many years of sustained development have been dramatic. In 1945, more than one third of France's labor force still worked the land; by 1980 the proportion had declined to 8 per cent, despite a steady rise in agricultural production. Towns and cities have burgeoned correspondingly — and not only to receive the influx of country-dwellers seeking a share of the expanding national wealth. The population, stagnant or declining in the early decades of the century, has been increasing without interruption since 1946, partly as a result of generous child allowances provided by the state and partly because of changes in social attitudes, from a near-despondent peasant conservatism to an optimistic, postwar confidence. The rate of increase peaked after the war; even in the 1980s, France's population continues to grow more quickly than most in the

In the Galeries Lafayette, one of Paris' biggest department stores, the central iron-and-glass cupola soars to a height of 132 feet over four stories of sales floors. Built in 1895, the dome is a showpiece of the Art Nouveau style.

European Economic Community (EEC). One major consequence has been to encourage the kind of urbanization that nations such as Britain, Germany and the United States attained a century or more before.

Nowhere have the changes been so apparent as in Paris. It has always been the center of France, not geographically — it is well to the north — but in every other way. It is the hub of the communications network of road, rail and waterway, the source of government and decision-making, and of course, the country's cultural showcase.

There is not one Paris, but two. Surrounding the historic inner city — *la ville de Paris* — is a wide ring of bedroom communities and industrial suburbs, which trace their origin back a century or so to France's last great phase of industrial expansion. For the most part, these consisted of the cheapest housing for the maximum number of workers; out of sight and out of mind of the "real" Paris, the *banlieue*, as the suburban ring was called, became a sort of dumping ground for everything that Paris proper could not or would not accommodate: industrial plants and gasworks, graveyards and junkyards, and of course a huge working population far outnumbering that of Paris itself.

Alarmed by the rate of growth in the 1950s — the population of the *banlieue* was increasing by 130,000 a year — the government began to take planning seriously. Five new towns, capable of absorbing most of the increase for decades to come, were created, and the thriving state of the national economy in the 1960s meant that money was available to furnish them with excellent facilities. They boast up-to-date hospitals, libraries, sports facilities and, above all, a transport system including

Two of the Parisian boulevards laid out by 19th Century planner Baron Haussmann stretch west from the Arc de Triomphe. On the left is the residential Avenue Foch; the Avenue de la Grande Armée leads to the high-rise business complex of La Défense.

the Réseau Express Régional, the "supermetro" to the suburbs that rivals the best the world has to offer.

The problems of the city itself were no less pressing. Despite a marked population loss since the war, inner Paris was grossly crowded. Its narrow streets were hopelessly choked with traffic, and a shortage of office space impeded its attempts to be a great European business capital. At the same time, because of its historic beauty, a program of ruthless demolition and rebuilding was out of the question.

Throughout the 1960s and 1970s, a debate raged between conservationists who felt that any major changes would destroy the city and reconstructionists who insisted that without immediate attention, Paris as a living town would die. The net result was a compromise that satisfied neither party in the end: Paris is still overcrowded and prone to traffic chaos, but its historic skyline is now punctuated by the tower blocks of the 20th Century. Still, Paris breathes more easily than it did, and it has suffered less from redevelopment than most other European capitals. Among the major changes were the building of the *périphérique* — the beltway, opened in 1970, that keeps all through traffic away from the city center — and the transfer of Les Halles, the huge complex of food markets through which a fifth of all of the country's produce is funneled, to a new site on the outskirts of the capital.

The greatest symbol of Parisian renewal, though, is perhaps the most controversial. The Pompidou Cultural Center, a brightly colored industrial-looking cube of a building, inspired shrieks of outrage from the moment its design was published. When it opened in 1977, it was compared to an oil refinery because of the maze of pipes and ducts carrying the power and heating systems, which its ultramodern architects had boldly exposed to view. The center still has enemies; but it is thriving, a magnet for the Paris young who are drawn as much by the spectacle of continuous street theater on the wide, paved area outside as by the library, galleries, museums and concert hall the bizarre building actually contains. It has life; the new France may lack some of the charm — and much of the placidity — of what it has replaced, but it need never fear stagnation.

Paris, though, is not France, however much Parisians may like to think it is. The capital — whether the Paris of the Fifth Republic, the Paris of Napoleon,

1

the Paris of the Revolution or the Paris of the Bourbons, the absolute monarchs of the old regime — has always seen itself as the head, the brains, the source and origin of a monolithic and homogeneous state. The provinces have a different view of things; and a look around them is the best guide to the general condition of the nation.

In the north, for example, you will find a race of beer-drinkers, working the intensively cultivated clay of the Flanders plain or else absorbed in the heavy industries around the city of Lille. The soil, the industry, the architecture and indeed the human stock are similar to those in Belgium, within whose territory the other part of Flanders falls. The "cockpit of Europe," Flanders has been called, a favorite theater of war for centuries; and the border is simply a line drawn on the map by history, not a geographical divide. It is a reminder, as the writer Sanche de Gramont put it, that France is only "one of several possible arrangements of Western Europe."

The region, formerly rich in coal, was in the sooty forefront of France's 19th Century industrialization, and the working out of the coal veins and the decline in demand for the steel and iron of the heavy industries that grew up around the mines have hit it hard. Unemployment is high. The north remains France's leading textile producer, making wool and weaving linen from local Flanders flax as well as milling jute and cotton imported through the ports of Dunkirk and Calais — but the textile industry too is in decline.

Farther south lie Picardy and Champagne, both largely agricultural. In Picardy, wheatfields are interspersed with sugar beets, potatoes and market gardens. As mechanization has taken the

work force from the fields, many have found jobs in the sugar refineries, canneries and food-processing plants that dot the countryside and cluster around the towns. In effect, Picardy is a continuation of the great Flanders plain. Its industries are smaller and more diverse, but the people and the landscape are the same, and so is its history of constant warfare and invasion. Place names here can still evoke a shudder: St. Quentin and Château-Thierry, a quiet little river called the Somme; hundreds of thousands of well-tended military tombstones still mark the harvest of World War I.

In adjacent Champagne, the bustle of producing the world's most famous wine draws more attention than anything else, although the area under vines is somewhat less than 1 per cent of the district's land. An average year sees the production of more than 150 million bottles of a wine that was almost worthless until the 17th Century, when in a kind of fairy tale, the monk Dom Pérignon discovered how to trap its wonderful effervescence. In the 18th Century, viticulture took its place with metallurgy and textiles among the region's main industries. Today, the Champagne trade centers around the gracious, largely 19th Century towns of Epernay and Reims; beyond them the countryside, once dry and infertile, has been transformed by energy and skill into a rich land, heavy with wheat.

Across the river Bresle from Picardy lies the old duchy of Normandy, named after the dynamic Norsemen who began to settle here in the Ninth Century. At first, they used the land as a base for inland forays (they almost captured Paris in 885); then they consolidated it into a realm that was strong enough to conquer England in 1066 (and far

more powerful than the nascent kingdom of France to the south). Now, the flat or gently rolling countryside has a pastoral air. Dense hedgerows enclose meadows or orchards, which yield the apples from which the wineless Normans produce their cider and their Calvados, a fiery apple brandy that mellows well with age. Butter and cheese are produced in great abundance.

The people are canny and self-contained, and their cooking, based largely upon cream and apples, is among the best in France. Blue eyes are not uncommon, but otherwise little trace remains of their Viking forebears. As everywhere in France, the peasantry has left the land in droves to seek a better future in industry, especially in eastern Normandy, where the great shipbuilding port of Le Havre and the manufacturing complex growing up around Rouen (the beautiful medieval city where Joan of Arc was burned in 1431), are both expanding rapidly.

Farther along the Atlantic coast is Brittany, perhaps the most distinctive of all French provinces. Brittany is France's Celtic fringe; ethnically, its people have much in common with the Cornish and Welsh across the English Channel, and a minority still speak the old Celtic tongue. Tourists in the summer months flock to its rugged, picturesque coasts, but inland Brittany is a harsh, windswept place, and until recently a poor one. It did not become part of the kingdom of France until as late as 1532, and its inhabitants have often wondered if the accession was their loss as much as France's gain.

Industry, as opposed to hard work, has never really established itself in Brittany, and even now provides employment for scarcely 20 per cent of the working population. Brittany has al-

PATTERNS OF SETTLEMENT

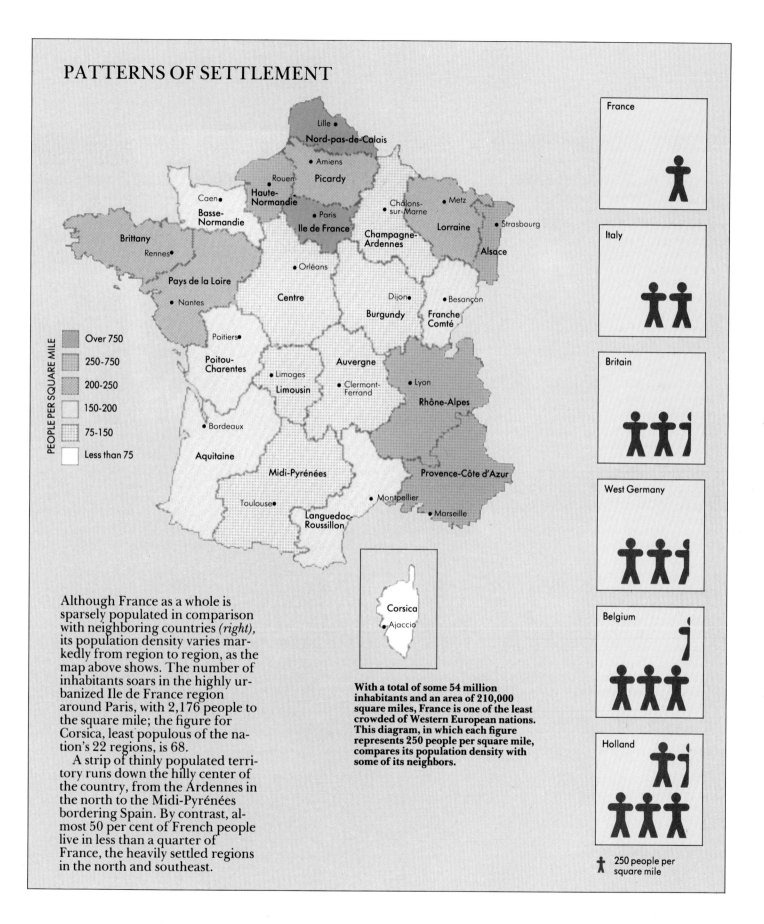

PEOPLE PER SQUARE MILE

- Over 750
- 250-750
- 200-250
- 150-200
- 75-150
- Less than 75

Lille
Nord-pas-de-Calais
Amiens
Rouen
Picardy
Caen
Haute-Normandie
Basse-Normandie
Paris
Ile de France
Châlons-sur-Marne
Metz
Lorraine
Strasbourg
Brittany
Rennes
Champagne-Ardennes
Alsace
Pays de la Loire
Orléans
Nantes
Dijon
Besançon
Centre
Burgundy
Franche-Comté
Poitiers
Poitou-Charentes
Auvergne
Limoges
Clermont-Ferrand
Lyon
Limousin
Rhône-Alpes
Bordeaux
Aquitaine
Midi-Pyrénées
Provence-Côte d'Azur
Toulouse
Montpellier
Languedoc-Roussillon
Marseille

Corsica
Ajaccio

France

Italy

Britain

West Germany

Belgium

Holland

250 people per square mile

Although France as a whole is sparsely populated in comparison with neighboring countries *(right)*, its population density varies markedly from region to region, as the map above shows. The number of inhabitants soars in the highly urbanized Ile de France region around Paris, with 2,176 people to the square mile; the figure for Corsica, least populous of the nation's 22 regions, is 68.

A strip of thinly populated territory runs down the hilly center of the country, from the Ardennes in the north to the Midi-Pyrénées bordering Spain. By contrast, almost 50 per cent of French people live in less than a quarter of France, the heavily settled regions in the north and southeast.

With a total of some 54 million inhabitants and an area of 210,000 square miles, France is one of the least crowded of Western European nations. This diagram, in which each figure represents 250 people per square mile, compares its population density with some of its neighbors.

23

ways been out of step with the rest of France. During the Revolution of 1789, the province was passionately royalist; throughout the secularizing 19th Century, it was enthusiastically Catholic. As outsiders, Bretons have provided a disproportionate number of France's soldiers and sailors, and, sadly, her emigrants: A large percentage of the settlers in French Canada were originally from Brittany.

There was little enough to keep them at home. The land was poor; their native Celtic culture was derided and their language virtually forbidden. Until recently, a Breton had to call himself by a recognized French Christian name, at least for official purposes: The national bureaucracy flatly ignored traditional Breton names and treated their owners as if they did not exist. But now things have changed. Government subsidies helped to revitalize the region's economy, and thanks to the determination of the educated young, Breton culture has undergone a revival. The language is also now tolerated, and can even be taught in school as a second tongue; but years of neglect have reduced its audience, and it remains to be seen whether the newly revived interest among the young will be enough to compensate for its decline among the peasantry, its traditional guardians. The Breton revival has also acquired a political dimension, with, predictably, a small underground "activist" wing that is prepared to use bombs to make its point.

François Argouache could be described as typifying the evolution of modern Brittany. Born in 1938, the son of small farmers at Morlaix near the northwest coast, he went to college, and now has a well-paying job running the economic development agency for this prosperous and dynamic part of the region. He and his Breton wife live in a neat house in the pretty fishing village of Carantec, and they have two teenage children in school.

Says Argouache: "As a child I learned Breton at home, for it was the language my parents used. But if I spoke it at school, the teacher would punish me by making me wear a fool's cap or he would have me run around the courtyard 20 times. Those were the orders from Paris. Today, all that has changed, the people are free to express their native culture as they wish." His children take their Breton identity for granted; ironically they feel less need to assert it than their father because it is no longer forbidden.

Argouache, who is adamantly opposed to the violent tactics of the separatist underground, is a supporter of autonomy for Brittany, a concept he carefully distinguishes from total independence, which he thinks would not make economic sense. Instead, he advocates a return to provincial government in the shape of a locally elected assembly with its own budget. Such a body was set up in 1972, with very limited powers, and Argouache sees as the way ahead a steady increase in its scope and means. When asked to define what it means to him to be Breton, he replies with an ambivalence shared by many of his compatriots: "Well, I also feel entirely French. But within France, Brittany has its own personality, history and culture. We have our own language, folk songs and dances, and I'm proud of the cultural revival that is now keeping these alive."

South of Brittany comes the country of the Loire, the mighty — but unnavigable — river flowing past the old royal province of La Vendée to emerge at the gracious, stately port of Nantes. Like nearby Brittany, La Vendée was staunchly royalist during the Revolution; the portable guillotines trundled down the roads from Paris and exacted a terrible revenge. Nantes itself, a great seaport, has always looked out toward the ocean rather than inland to Paris. Much of its early prosperity was built upon the slave trade, and when the Revolutionary Convention in Paris in 1794 pronounced its Declaration of the Rights of Man, the hardheaded Nantes slavers simply ignored its provisions as so much Parisian hot air and carried on their grisly trade. The port still thrives, though less disreputably.

Upstream, the Loire, its banks heavy with vineyards, flows through Anjou and Touraine, ancient provinces that are now swallowed up in the modern regions of Pays de la Loire and Centre. This is the "garden of France," studded with the châteaux that are the area's great tourist attraction. Chambord, with some 440 rooms, is the largest; but possibly the most beautiful of them all is Chenonceaux, built out across a river, a magical example of French Renaissance exuberance.

Looping upward, the Loire passes through some of the most fertile land in Europe, to Orléans. Northwest of Orléans lies the great plain of the Beauce, a seemingly illimitable sea of wheat and corn from which the twin towers of Chartres's great cathedral rise as if forced from the soil by the same germinal power that pushes up the wheat. It was in the Beauce that the great 19th Century writer Émile Zola set his novel *La Terre — The Earth —* a depiction of the brutality, lust and violence of peasant life. It shocked all France. But the Beauce has changed since Zola's time: Its population has diminished and the farms of those remaining have been consolidated and become mechanized, more of a business than a way of life.

Below the Loire country is the old province of Aquitaine, a huge territory with a gentle Atlantic climate. It is celebrated above all for the great vineyards

around Bordeaux, but the region also grows much of France's black tobacco as well as a proportion of almost every other kind of agricultural produce. South of the Gironde estuary, where Bordeaux nestles sheltered from the sea, the coastal plain is flat and sandy. Known as the Landes, the area was once a wasteland, but careful planting has made of it one of Europe's largest pine forests; the coast itself boasts mile upon mile of beaches of light-colored sand that in summer attract vacationers by the thousands and have earned it the title *Côte d'Argent* — or silver coast.

In the south, the land slopes upward to the Pyrenees and the Basque country, a land of chalet-shaped houses with red beams crisscrossing white-washed walls and gently sloping roofs of bright red tiles. The Basque people are a European enigma. They live on both sides of the Franco-Spanish border, yet by ethnic origin they are neither French nor Spanish and speak a unique language related to no known tongue. In Spain, a militant separatist movement has for years been fighting for independence from the authorities in Madrid; the less numerous French

Basques are more quiescent although just as aware of their cultural identity, content to help their cousins across the Pyrenees with arms smuggling and a shelter for hunted refugees.

Inland along the mountains is the modern region of Midi-Pyrénées, which, with the adjacent Languedoc-Roussillon, curling around the Mediterranean Sea past Montpellier, is really the historic land of Languedoc. For the most part, the country is hot, dry and hilly; along the Mediterranean coast are planted some of France's most productive vineyards, the source of

Cyclists competing in the Tour de France fill the main street of Orbec in Normandy, while a line of service cars waits to follow them.

much of the nation's everyday drinking wine. The region takes its name from the language once spoken throughout southern France — the language of *oc*. *Oc* meant yes; *langue d'oc* was a convenient, shorthand term to distinguish both the southern region and its dialect from *langue d'oïl*, the rest of France, where yes was signified by *oïl* or *oui*. As in Brittany, the old tongue has in the present century been dying out; again as in Brittany, local patriots are trying to revive it, but its long-term future remains in doubt.

Inland from Languedoc is the Massif Central, one seventh of the area of France and the country's stony heart. Geologically, the hills and mountains of the Massif are old, as old as anything in Europe; but the colossal uplifting of the Alps a few million years ago (the day before yesterday, in geological terms) tilted and cracked the old granite, triggering volcanoes and twisting the landscape so that fierce new rivers sprang into being and tore deep gorges from the ancient rock. The old volcanoes and gorges are the land's most distinctive feature today. The Auvergne, at the center of the Massif Central, is noted for its *puys* — precipitous studs of rock, the granitic core plugs of volcanoes whose cones have eroded away — and *cirques* — volcanic craters, sometimes filled with water. The gorges of the main rivers — to the west, the Dordogne and Lot, to the south, the Ardèche and Tarn — are awe-inspiring. They are spanned nowadays by dizzying viaducts and bridges, but in the past they were formidable obstacles to communication, and contributed greatly to the region's isolation.

The land is beautiful, but bleak; the high plateaus are often under snow for months in winter, and living has always been hard. Predictably, the population in the area has been decreasing for a century, as its peasants looked for a better life elsewhere. Surprisingly, the Auvergne boasts one large industrial city, Clermont-Ferrand, with tire manufacturers and textile and printing works; but most of the region's emigrants have settled further afield in Lyon and in the growing suburbs around Paris.

To come from the rugged Massif Central into the Rhône Valley and Provence, especially in winter, is to experience something like rebirth. Provence is above all else a land of light; a region of olives and vines, warmth and sunshine, the true Mediterranean France. It has a long history; Provence was one of the first acquisitions of the expanding Roman Empire, and much Roman architecture remains, especially in the old imperial capital of Arles. When Rome fell, Provence was still rich and prosperous and, as such, the target for a succession of more or less devastating invasions; the last group of invaders — Arabs who came swarming through North Africa and Spain — were not displaced until the 10th Century. Provence then enjoyed almost 500 years of

THE GREATEST SHOW ON WHEELS

Ever since its inception in 1903, the Tour de France has been the foremost cycling event in Europe. The first race drew 60 entrants and a large crowd at the start outside Paris. Now it is a media extravaganza watched by hundreds of thousands of roadside spectators and a television audience numbering tens of millions.

From late June to mid-July, some 130 bicyclists strain to complete a circuit of nearly 2,400 miles. The route is changed each year and encompasses many landscapes, including mountain passes in the Alps and Pyrenees as well as the flatter terrain of northern France. Sometimes it incorporates short detours into neighboring countries such as Belgium or Spain; invariably it ends in Paris, with a furious sprint up the Champs Élysées to a finish line near the Arc de Triomphe.

Competitors belong to teams, each 10 strong, from such bicycle-crazy countries as France itself, Italy, Belgium, Spain and Holland. The team sponsors — cycling firms, soft-drink manufacturers and the like — provide bicycles and spare parts as well as motorized backup personnel, including mechanics and masseurs. Service vehicles carry these aides, along with doctors, race officials and journalists, in the wake of the riders as they sweep along country roads.

The Tour is organized in a succession of daily stages, up to a maximum of 22, which vary in length from less than 90 to 180 miles. Certain days just have time trials — shorter stages with staggered starts against the clock.

The race has two scoring systems, one based on points — awarded for positions in each day's race — and the other on race times. The leader in the points table is identified each day by a green jersey — a coveted honor in its own right, but little more than a consolation prize in comparison with the kudos associated with the yellow jersey. It is worn by the rider with the best cumulative time at the end of the race: the overall winner.

The rewards for the victor include cash and goods, but these cannot compare with the adulation of the crowds, which makes a hero of every winner and turns French champions such as Louison Bobet, Jacques Anquetil and Bernard Hinault into celebrities, second only to presidents in renown.

1

At a fish market in the Breton port of Concarneau, buyers from local hotels scrutinize the morning's haul while an auctioneer calls their bids. With over 600 miles of Atlantic coastline, Brittany is France's leading deep-sea fishing region, providing over a third of its annual catch.

independence before it was united under the French crown in 1486. Like their neighbors to the west, the people of Provence used to speak a version of the old *langue d'oc.* A substantial literature exists in the Provençal tongue, which since the 19th Century has experienced something of a revival.

Provence is not all rich: Inland, the countryside is an arid maze of scrub-covered hills, and two thirds of the region's population live in a narrow strip along the coast, where the climate is almost subtropical. All over this area are found lone farmsteads, with walls of local stone that is white or pale gold and roofs made of terra-cotta tiles of a mellow pinkish brown, standing next to slender cypresses — the archetypal, sun-parched Provençal scene that Van Gogh and Cézanne used to paint. The only drawback is the *mistral* — a savage wind, funneled down the Rhône Valley by the mountains on either side, which can be powerful enough to annihilate crops and flatten trees.

Near the mouth of the Rhône is Provence's biggest city, Marseille, which vies with Lyon for the title of France's second largest city; certainly it is the nation's busiest port, second only to Rotterdam in the European Community. To the east, from beyond Toulon to the Italian border, lies the fabled Côte d'Azur, the French Riviera, centered around the cities of Nice and Cannes. Rampant development has destroyed a great deal of its charm, but the ugly concrete buildings that barricade the shore have not disturbed the glorious Mediterranean weather, and vacationers arrive by the thousands.

Nice itself and the land around it has only been French since 1860, when it was ceded by the Kingdom of Sardinia to the Emperor Napoleon III as the price of his support in the struggle for Italian independence. After France's defeat in 1940, Nice was occupied briefly by Mussolini's Italian troops; perhaps as a result of that experience, its people have since shown no desire to be anything other than French.

The inhabitants of the Côte d'Azur are a favored race, and are very aware of their privileged situation. One such is Jacques Cornet, a bank employee in his early 30s. Born in Antibes, he still lives there with his wife and two children, aged eight and 10, in an apartment he is buying with the aid of a loan from his employer. He commutes to work every day in the industrial complex at Sophia Antipolis, a high-technology development three miles outside Antibes that has been christened the Silicon Valley of the Riviera.

He finds the lifestyle of Provence and the Riviera relaxed and comfortable. Whether drinking aperitifs on a café terrace or playing *boules* in a tree-shaded square, the local people, he claims, are less hectically concerned with work than other Frenchmen and devote more attention to leisure. For him that means particularly his new passion, windsurfing; the climate encourages outdoor sports, and M. Cornet, a dapper figure in immaculate white jeans and short-sleeved sports shirt, keeps himself fit and trim.

M. Cornet believes that he could probably earn more money up in the north, but that would not compensate for losing the pleasures of Riviera living. His children would no longer be able to go out bicycling in the evenings after school for much of the year, as

28

they can in Antibes. And the family could no longer take weekend trips to the Maritime Alps, just an hour's drive away, where M. Cornet can indulge his other hobby, mountaineering. As he himself puts it, "There's a quality of life down here that you can't really find anywhere else in France."

The classic route northward from Provence is up the valley of the Rhône toward Lyon. Here Roman legionaires built the first great roads by which they conquered Gaul and here, today, the *autoroute* to Paris runs; the hurried traveler can hurtle through the Lyonnais countryside as if it did not exist. It is a pity to do so. Lyon itself is a beautiful city, the core of a great industrial suburb and the gastronomic capital of France — no mean achievement in a country that everywhere prides itself on the quality of its food.

The whole Rhône Valley is lined with vineyards as far as Lyon; then the river's course turns east toward Lake Geneva, twisting through the Alpine country north of the dynamic city of Grenoble. Much of the French Alps were part of the territory of the old duchy of Savoy, and did not become French until 1860. The change made little difference to the people: Mountaineers had trouble enough to make a living in their high valleys without worrying unduly about political allegiances. Now the huge popularity of winter sports has brought an unprecedented influx of visitors to the area, and its prosperity matches its beauty.

North of Lyon, the river Saône leads into the heart of Burgundy, through villages and districts whose very names are enough to set one reaching for a corkscrew: first the Beaujolais, then Mâcon, then past Chalon and Beaune and the slopes of the Côte d'Or. Bur-

A GASTRONOME'S DELIGHT

Of all the foods for which France is famous, none has more bizarre origins than *foie gras* ("fatty liver"), a fashionable delicacy since the late 18th Century. Produced between October and April, this specialty of Alsace and Périgord involves force-feeding geese for five to six weeks on corn. The bird's liver increases three or four times and can weigh up to four pounds.

After the bird is slaughtered, the liver is removed and prepared in numerous ways: poached, puréed into a mousse or made into the famed *pâté de foie gras*, a paste of cooked livers delicately flavored with wine, aromatics and truffles. Although some 1,000 tons of the delicacy are produced each year, the supply fails to meet demands; as a result, duck livers are sometimes prepared in the same way, and 1,000 tons are imported annually, principally from Hungary.

A goose is force-fed from a machine.

Geese raised for *foie gras* are herded by their owner outside his château in Périgord.

gundy is far north for red wine country, and only the most intensive labor in the vineyards makes production possible at all. Most holdings are very small: The countryside is a patchwork of tiny vineyards, each of them tended jealously by their owners.

Burgundy's people tend to be jovial and stubbornly independent, with a strong fatalistic streak that comes of sometimes seeing an entire harvest ruined by one of the region's frequent September hailstorms. The traditional houses are odd edifices, with the cellar built first as their centerpiece, and the living quarters added on top. Dijon, the regional capital, was once the seat of dukes more powerful than the kings of France; now it is a quiet and elegant

provincial city and cultural center.

To the east lies the old province of Franche-Comté, annexed by France in the 17th Century, and the Jura Mountains, geologically the most recent in the country, whose quiet valleys have been largely untouched by the encroaching 20th Century.

To the north, Alsace and Lorraine, completing the circuit of France, have had a much more troubled history. Alsace, sandwiched between the Vosges Mountains and the Rhine River, has been German almost as long as it has been French during the last century, and most of its inhabitants still speak a dialect of their own that is closely related to German. Fittingly, the Alsatian capital of Strasbourg, whose ownership

was once so bitterly disputed, became in 1949 the meeting-place of the Council of Europe and is now the principal seat of the European Parliament, symbol of European unity. Such status, however, does have its drawbacks: Strasbourg's inhabitants complain of the high rents and unseemly night life that the EEC has brought to a city that was for most of its history a placid backwater.

Neighboring Lorraine has also been a point of contention between France and Germany; the graveyards around Verdun, last resting-place of hundreds of thousands of men, are a chilling reminder of the cost of territorial conflict. Agriculturally, Lorraine is less rich than other regions of France; but its coal and minerals account for its desirability and former wealth. It is not so wealthy now: The iron and steel industries are in deep decline. Unemployment levels are among the highest in the country, and steel towns such as Longwy on the Belgian border have been reduced to miserable shadows of their former selves.

The problems of Corsica, last of the French regions, are more particular. This huge Mediterranean island, 3,480 square miles in extent, lies some 100 miles to the southeast of Nice and closer to the Tuscan shore of Italy. It has only been part of France since 1769, and Corsicans retain a certain ambivalence toward their status. On the one hand, there is a strong tradition of independence that manifests itself today in a small but violent separatist movement.

The bomb throwers would never achieve a majority in an election; but they have found enough support among their notoriously close-mouthed fellow islanders to make it hard for the authorities to suppress them. On the other hand, there is a rival Corsican tradition of seeking one's fortune on the mainland: Napoleon Bonaparte was not the first Corsican to make his name in Paris, nor the last. As things stand now, Corsicans make up a remarkable 15 per cent of France's policemen, and it is often darkly suggested that they provide at least as high a proportion of the nation's criminals. Certainly, Corsicans are famously tough: The island was the first part of France to liberate itself from German occupation in World War II, and that with little outside assistance.

As if variety within her European borders was not enough, France still has a scattering of outposts around the world. There are five overseas departments: Guadeloupe and Martinique in the Caribbean, French Guiana on the South American mainland, Réunion, east of Madagascar in the Indian Ocean, and St. Pierre and Miquelon, islands south of Newfoundland in the North Atlantic. Each of them sends deputies to the National Assembly in Paris, though they have local assemblies of their own with wide powers over finance and administration. In addition, five overseas territories include islands in the South Pacific, the Indian Ocean and portions of Antarctica.

Diversity succeeds diversity: In the end, perhaps the most remarkable fact about France is not the great range of dissimilarities that mark as separate her provinces and their peoples, but the country's very existence as a stable and united nation. Why France at all, and not some quite different arrangement of borders and frontiers? What links together this unruly variety? For the most part, the answer is to be found in language and in culture, and in the shared experience that forged them into a binding force.

The beginnings of France as a nation state are generally traced back to the election of Hugh Capet as King of France in 987 A.D. by the powerful dukes and feudal magnates who actually ruled the territory. The barons had no intention of creating a real and functioning royal power; that was why they chose Capet, who, as ruler only of the tiny region of the Ile de France around the scruffy little town of Paris, was weaker than most of his ostensibly subject lords. The fact that the language used in the Capetian domain was an obscure dialect of the *langue d'oïl* called Francien, rather than a far more widely spoken language such as Norman or Occitan, may have helped to clinch Hugh Capet's election as king. The great dukes expected little trouble from their royal master.

They were spectacularly wrong. The history of the succeeding centuries — recounted in more detail in Chapter Two — is the story of how Capet's fragile dynasty and its collateral descendants grew gradually in influence and strength, until by the 16th Century France had acquired an absolute monarchy. And as the monarchy grew, so did the French language that was associated with it.

The spread of the language was slow at first. In the 11th and 12th Centuries, most official documents were still written in Latin, and most vernacular literature used one of the southern dialects. By the 13th Century, however, the developing Francien dialect had become the language of administration, and it never looked back. For centuries to come, the nation's peasant majority continued to speak their own, mutually incomprehensible tongues; but the language that ruled them all was French, and anyone who sought advancement had to learn it.

The heyday of the French language, in the 17th and the 18th Centuries, coincided with the peak of French military, economic and diplomatic power. To French satisfaction, it was adopted by the educated elites of other countries, most notably in Germany, Austria and Russia. It became the language of diplomacy, the language in which treaties were written and notes exchanged between great powers. In France itself, it became the object of an interest that amounted almost to veneration. The author Antoine de Rivarol, in his book *On the Universality of the French Language* published shortly before the Revolution, summed up a widespread convic-

A mime amiably parodies a chic passerby to the amusement of customers sitting in an outdoor café in the Mediterranean resort of St. Tropez. Once a quiet fishing village, St. Tropez became a mecca for sunlovers and draws 50,000 visitors a year.

1

tion when he wrote, *"Ce qui n'est pas clair, n'est pas français."* That which is not clear, is not French.

At the time Rivarol wrote, the French he was describing was spoken by only a minority of his own countrymen. It took the Revolution, the advent of mass conscription and above all the rise of popular education during the 19th Century before the average Gascon had learned enough of the universal tongue to converse freely with the average Lyonnais. And while the peasantry of France was learning French, the rest of the world was forgetting it. Whatever the old aristocracies had spoken, it became clear that in the modern world a patriotic German would use German; a Russian, Russian. Worse still from the French point of view, English was fast becoming the world language of science and commerce; in the 20th Century, for the first time, perhaps, since the days of Hugh Capet, French is on the defensive.

In fact, French is still a major world language, and is likely to remain so. It is the 12th most common tongue in the world and only half its speakers live in France. Apart from French Canada, a large proportion of emergent Africa uses it as a lingua franca; francophone regions in Asia and the Pacific mark the extent of France's former colonial empire. Nevertheless, the French people — at least, the officials among them — feel their language is under threat, and they have taken up arms to beat off what they consider to be a wave of barbarous neologisms from the old rival, English: words described, with barbed humor, as *franglais*.

Words such as *le cocktail* and *le weekend* have been around for long enough to cause no offense; but a deluge of new forms such as *le marketingman* provoked

Watching the world from her home in Finistère, a Breton woman sports the region's traditional black dress and apron, worn with clogs and a black cap. Satin or velvet aprons and lace headdresses, once regular attire for Sundays and market days, are now kept mainly for special occasions.

a law, passed in 1977 with the consent of all parties, that insists on the use of French in all advertisements, official documents and even on the radio and television, and French French at that. Most outsiders would be sympathetic. Many other languages have been disfigured by ugly English and American-English neologisms, including English and American-English themselves. What is surprising to a foreigner, however, is the centralized, official nature of the French response, an indication that the French language is still seen as a thing in some sense apart from the French people, a tool of government that must be maintained, in pristine condition, by the governors.

French culture, the other element of the binding web, is both more powerful and less well defined than the language

from which it largely springs. Certainly it is less susceptible to even the pretense of a centralized control. On the one hand, French culture means the great tradition of French philosophy and literature, itself a coalition of opposites: the cool rationalism of the philosophers Descartes and Voltaire with the passion of the Romantics, Rousseau and Hugo. On the other, it calls to mind a deep and often energetic concern with the quality of life: a sense of style, whether expressed through flair in clothes and design, or in a love for good food and wine; in either case, the approach is not casual, but involves the taking of infinite pains.

All Frenchmen have it, this thing called style, or believe they have; all French speakers aspire to it; and the rest of the world, with France before them as example, can admire it. An old

joke claimed that Paris was where good Americans went when they died; the germ of truth, which perhaps provoked the laughter, is that France does offer something of an *au-delà* — a hereafter — to its admirers and its own people alike. For an integral part of the real France is the dream of France that it includes and by which it is in turn included, the ideal that animates and ennobles the reality. Perhaps that is the reason why so many outsiders look with alarm and dread on any changes: A dream should be immutable.

In fact, the changes to the country have not been slight: In 40 years, France has undergone a remarkable transformation. It has experienced a period of astonishing growth, in the course of which three quarters of its remaining peasantry have moved from the country to the booming cities. In

many respects, it has become simply another highly competitive Western nation, with all the brashness of the late 20th Century. Advertisements for company executives in the Paris press call out for *jeunes loups* — young wolves — and France's wolfish businessmen can howl as loudly and as greedily as their counterparts in New York or London.

Yet it is hard to believe that France will ever be swallowed up in some bland, transatlantic Western world. It guards its independence far too jealously for that. True, it sacrificed a measure of that independence when it became, in 1957, a founding member of the European Economic Community. But the rewards in terms of prosperity have been immense, and the sacrifice of sovereignty very small. In its defense policy too, France — to the frequent annoyance of its allies — has remained

very much its own master. Although nominally still a member of NATO, it withdrew its forces from the organization's unified command in 1966, and it maintains at considerable expense the *force de frappe* — its own nuclear deterrent. To France's NATO allies, it has often seemed that the country is trying to have its cake and eat it, too. To the French, such a policy is only logical: They have never been afraid to live with contradictions.

Indeed, France in the 1980s is very much a land of contradictions, where tradition and modernity live together in a state of unwed coexistence that necessity compels. One example, extreme but not untypical, may show the kind of balance that has been struck. The sleepy little town of Pauillac, near Bordeaux, is the source of some of France's greatest wine: Three of the five most highly rated clarets come from its few square miles of vineyards, sloping gently to the estuary of the Gironde. Now, gleaming on the outskirts of the town, there stands a great new oil refinery. It was not built without strong local opposition, and in a nation with a less powerful central government, it might not have been built at all. It is not attractive, but it serves the new France, pumping the industrial lifeblood to which it owes its wealth. Meanwhile, only a few hundred yards away, the slow and patient work continues in the vineyard, much as it has done for centuries. The wine continues to mature in the cool silence of the châteaux' cellars, and when it is sold it will fetch high prices: Bordeaux is still considered the best wine in the world. Continuity and change coexist side by side — a fitting image for a country that is trying to preserve the best of the old as it energetically explores the new. □

VISTAS OF A DIVERSE LAND

Other countries may boast of more grandiose physical features, but no other European nation has such a concentration of diverse landscapes as France. Every kind of scenery other than that of the tropics or the steppes can be found here, compressed into a country smaller in area than Texas.

France owes its scenic variety to its position, midway between the Pole and the Equator at the junction of three climate zones—the oceanic, continental and Mediterranean. In the north and west, the Atlantic's benign maritime influence tempers the harsher winds that blow from the European landmass to the east, and in the south, the fortunate regions of Languedoc and Provence bask in dry heat.

Overlaid on the landscape is a tracery of human occupation as dense and differentiated as the topography that supports it. The product of some 5,000 years of continuous cultivation, this man-made geography, ranging from vast grainfields through vineyards and olive groves to barren sheep pastures, now forms a natural heritage as precious as the land itself.

Against a background of storm clouds, a ray of sunlight pinpoints the citadel of Calvi in northern Corsica, France's Mediterranean "mountain in the sea." The rugged relief protects large parts of the island as a wilderness, creating a bastion against mainland influences.

34

Sea-carved chalk stacks, arches and coves on Normandy's 90-mile-long "alabaster coast" recede into the misty distance near Étretat.

From a tight nucleus of dwellings, a patchwork of unenclosed fields in central France's Touraine Valley stretches to the horizon. Strip cultivation is disappearing because of a government-sponsored scheme that helps farmers to regroup scattered properties through land exchanges.

Lying several feet below high water level, the coastal marshes at Guérande, north of the Loire estuary, are one of three centers of salt production on the Atlantic coast. Sea water is channeled first into evaporating basins, then into rows of pans *(center, foreground)*, where the salt accumulates.

A hamlet huddles under clouds in the foothills of the Pyrenees. In the harsh winter, herdsmen took sheep and goats from such settlements to the lowland plains to graze. The pastoral life is now in decline, and many communities have been depopulated or invaded by vacation-home buyers.

A backdrop of mountains, including the 13,596-foot Aiguille Verte *(below, right)*, dwarfs Chamonix, a famous resort in the French Alps. Resting in the shadow of Mont Blanc — at 15,840 feet, Europe's highest mountain — Chamonix also has its most elevated cable car, reaching 12,540 feet.

In a quintessentially Provençal scene, the ruins of a medieval church overlook the terracotta roofs of Collobrières, inland from St. Tropez.

A 264-foot-high granitic mound, capped by a 10th Century chapel, rises in the heart of Le Puy in the hilly Auvergne region of central France. The town takes its name from the local word for these cores of hard stone — the eroded remnants of extinct volcanoes.

CENTURIES OF GLORY AND REVOLT

A 15th Century German tapestry shows Joan of Arc being greeted at Chinon in 1429 by the Dauphin Charles, whose belief in his right to the French throne was restored by the shepherd girl's visions. Joan won from the future King an army and raised the English siege of Orléans.

All nations are the creations of history, and nowhere is this more evident than in France. The history of this great country is a story of growth and consolidation, the gradual molding of a unified nation-state from a heterogeneous collection of peoples. Even now, the garment of national unity is more a patchwork than a seamless cloak, and the nation's frontiers reflect not so much the barriers of nature as the outermost extensions of political will.

The first chapters in the story of French civilization belong in the realm of painting and sculpture — a fitting beginning for a culture traditionally preeminent in the fine arts. The people who inhabited southwestern France about 20,000 years ago left behind powerful works of art in the lifelike wild bulls, horses and reindeer painted on the walls of the caves of Lascaux, Les Eyzies, Trois Frères and a dozen others. Historians believe such painting was a magical activity, intended to give the tribe power over their quarry when they went hunting. Physically these Cro-Magnon men and women (the name, used to describe a tall, broadfaced Stone Age race, is that of a cave in the Dordogne district of southern France where they once lived) were little different from the people who now inhabit the same valleys.

The next peoples to leave substantial remnants of their culture in what we now call France were the builders of enormous stone monuments that still dot the landscape, especially in Brittany. They carved stones into cyclopean dolmens and menhirs, which are believed to have served as a means of forecasting the rising and setting of the moon at critical times of the agricultural year, when they needed the information for crop-sowing purposes.

Later, during the first millennium B.C., the megalith-builders were supplanted by a people possessing great metallurgical skills, the Celts, whose civilization eventually covered northern Europe from the Carpathians to Ireland. In Gaul, as Celtic France came to be known, their lords ruled over villages and farming estates, but the various tribes never cooperated sufficiently to form a unified state.

The Celts left no written accounts of themselves or their customs — but the Greeks and Romans took an interest in these ferocious and bibulous contemporaries. "The Gauls," noted Diodorus of Sicily in the 1st Century B.C., "are exceedingly addicted to the use of wine, and fill themselves with the wine which is brought into their country by merchants, drinking it unmixed."

Inevitably, these people came into conflict with the expanding empires of the Mediterranean. The port city of Massilia — today's Marseille — had been founded about 600 B.C. by Greek traders and colonists from the Ionian city of Phocea, in what is now Turkish Asia Minor. Their descendants supplied the Gauls with wine and they

43

2

helped the Romans in their war against Carthage. In turn, the Romans first came to Gaul in 154 B.C. as allies of the Massiliots in their campaigns against the local tribes at Nice and Antibes.

A century later, in 58 B.C., Julius Caesar gained command of the Roman forces in Gaul. With a far smaller but well-disciplined force, he thwarted a threatened invasion by more than 300,000 Helvetii — Celts from Switzerland — and then set about occupying the whole of Gaul. It was to remain a Roman province for nearly 500 years.

Roman Gaul was in many ways the matrix for the future nation of France. The Romans gave Gaul the Latin language as a lingua franca for administration, a legal system for the whole country, a set of weights and measures and a frontier that is still, approximately, that of modern France. They ruled the province from Lugdunum, modern Lyon, at the confluence of the Rhône and the Saône Rivers. With subsidies from, among others, Nero and Trajan, it became one of the most splendid cities of the empire.

Gaul under the Romans was well provided with schools and libraries, theaters, hot baths, swimming pools and other comforts. No longer were the Gauls dependent on imported wines for their favorite beverage. Ausonius, the 4th Century Gallo-Roman poet, prided himself on his vineyard in the Bordeaux region — a domain of 1,000 acres that still produces one of the best St. Émilion clarets.

Yet even as he was writing, the barbarians were, literally, at the gates. In 406 A.D. a horde of invaders crossed the Rhine River and pillaged 45 Gallo-Roman towns; before long they had overrun the entire northern region as far as Brittany. Shortly afterward, in 410 A.D., Rome was sacked by the Goths and the empire disintegrated. Out of the funeral pyre of Roman Gaul emerged a new order, ruled by fierce warrior tribes speaking Teutonic tongues, their breath smelling of leeks and their hair of the rancid butter that they used as a pomade.

The new lords saw themselves as successors to the Romans, and adopted their titles, customs and Christian religion. The Frankish king, Clovis, who occupied Paris in 486 A.D., assumed the title and costume of a Roman consul when he made his ceremonial entry into the city. His descendants — the Merovingians named after Merovig, founder of the dynasty — retained the crown until the 8th Century, when the last of the line was deposed by Pepin, regent of Neustria (in northwestern France), Burgundy and Provence and the father of Charlemagne.

Charlemagne was the first monarch to rule over the whole of France (except for Brittany, an irreducible bastion of unconquered Celts). He was crowned in 768 at Noyon, about 60 miles northeast of Paris. Although his birthplace is unknown, his origins and language were Teutonic, and as Karl der Grosse he figures as prominently in German as in French history. His favorite residence — later the site of his tomb — was at Aachen in Germany.

His armies conquered virtually the whole of Western Europe, from Brindisi, near the heel of the Italian boot, to Hamburg on the Elbe, and from the Carinthian Alps to the Pyrenees. To set the Church's seal on his achievement, Pope Leo III took the momentous step of crowning him "Roman emperor" in St. Peter's basilica on Christmas Day of the year 800. Until then, only the Byzantine emperors of distant Constan-

A gold reliquary, commissioned in 1481 by Louis XI, houses a fragment of the armbone of Charlemagne — king of the Franks in 768 and Holy Roman Emperor in 800. Successive French kings commemorated his feat of uniting present-day France, except Brittany, under one monarch.

44

tinople had dared to call themselves successors to the Caesars.

After his death in 814, Charlemagne was succeeded by his son, who ruled the vast empire until 843. When he died, the empire was divided among his heirs, and his father's precious heritage of a united Europe was destroyed. Yet Charlemagne was a larger-than-life figure whose character and accomplishments soon became the stuff of poetry and legend. As the peace and harmony of his reign faded into history, he was idealized in legends as the just and wise ruler protecting Christendom against its enemies. He was credited with superhuman powers, even a life after death. One tale had it that he waited, crowned and armed, to go forth with his knights and do battle for the faith on the day when the Antichrist should appear; another held that in years of good harvest he would ride over the Rhine River on a bridge of gold to bless the crops. His idealized image — and that of his faithful paladin, horn-blowing Roland — inspired the courts of France long after his real achievements were forgotten.

The quarrels and conflicts among Charlemagne's descendants weakened their defenses against Norwegian and Danish raiders — Norsemen, or Normans — who came swarming off their long ships to ravage the French coast during the Ninth Century. A contemporary chronicler described them as men of great cunning, avid for gain and for power, both lavish and greedy, and much to be feared since they were indifferent to every hardship. They came to plunder, but stayed to settle the lower valleys of the Seine, ceded to them as the duchy of Normandy in the 10th Century. Thus a new and essentially foreign element was added to what had

become a jigsaw puzzle of feudal French states, most of them owing only nominal allegiance to Charlemagne's heirs, the kings of France.

For several centuries, the dukes of Normandy pursued their separate destinies. In 1066, the illegitimate son of Duke Robert the Devil and a tanner's daughter took his army across the English Channel, won the Battle of Hastings, and, as William the Conqueror, was crowned king of England at Westminster. He spent much of his remaining 21 years in Normandy, and was buried in Caen. Subsequent English kings were to claim half of France as their hereditary domain, and their French possessions remained a bone of contention for 500 years. Calais, the last English stronghold in France, was not relinquished until 1558.

The kings of France, meanwhile, had lost most of their power to the regional lords, who ruled great duchies like those of Burgundy and Aquitaine, or counties, like those of Poitou, Blois, Anjou and Auvergne. Though Hugh Capet had been crowned "king of the Franks" in 987, the fealty due to him was tenuous. The powerful dukes and counts ruled their lands as independent fiefs, and intermittent warfare with their neighbors was regarded as a kind of universal sport.

To a 12th Century poet-nobleman like Bertran de Born, lord of Hautefort in Périgord, war was a "joyful season" when he could enjoy the sight of "tents and rich pavilions pitched, lances shattered, shields pierced, shining helmets split, and blows exchanged in battle." In one of his troubadour poems, he boasts of his plan to ride into battle under the walls of Périgueux, armed with a mace and sword, "And if I find some fat Poitevin he'll see how my sword cuts and on his head I'll make a mash of chain mail and brains."

For centuries, the Capet dynasty struggled to assert their authority over these fractious and belligerent vassals. Their own power base, the landlocked Ile de France, included not much more than Paris, Senlis and Orléans and the territory between them, but it lay astride the great rivers and trade routes of the north, and proved to be a strategic point of departure from which to undertake the reunification of the whole of France. Progress was slow and many setbacks were suffered; but gradually the pieces of the kingdom began to fall into place. In the 13th Century, King Philip Augustus succeeded in breaking the power of the English kings in France, and seized Normandy, Maine, Touraine, Anjou and the Auvergne. It was he who expanded Paris into a spacious and well-defended capital, constructing walls around the city

AN ENDURING TESTAMENT OF FAITH

Built on a commanding height in the Loire Valley, Chartres Cathedral is the crowning achievement of High Gothic — the soaring style of medieval church architecture marked by the use of the pointed arch and a profusion of stained-glass windows and sculptures. Consecrated in 1260 after a fire had destroyed most of an earlier structure, the building has been described as a "bible in stone"; its spires, rising as a testament of faith, are visible from miles away.

Despite its massive proportions, the interior of the cathedral is surprisingly light and airy — an effect Gothic architects achieved by the use of external buttresses. By doing away with the need for heavy roof supports inside the church, the buttresses made it possible to build higher and to open up the walls to a degree never attempted before.

Freed of some of their load-bearing duties, the walls served to frame what is perhaps Chartres's chief glory — the stained-glass windows that glow within it like transparent illuminated manuscripts. Roughly half of the windows were donated by members of the aristocracy; the rest were the gifts of merchant guilds, each one identified by a small, lifelike vignette, incorporated into the design, which illustrates its line of business *(opposite page, below)*.

From the northeast, the airy spires of Chartres Cathedral rise like a ship's masts above the roofs of the city.

With a delicacy that belies their massive proportions, arched columns frame the south transept's Rose Window and lancets, donated by a count of Dreux and his wife.

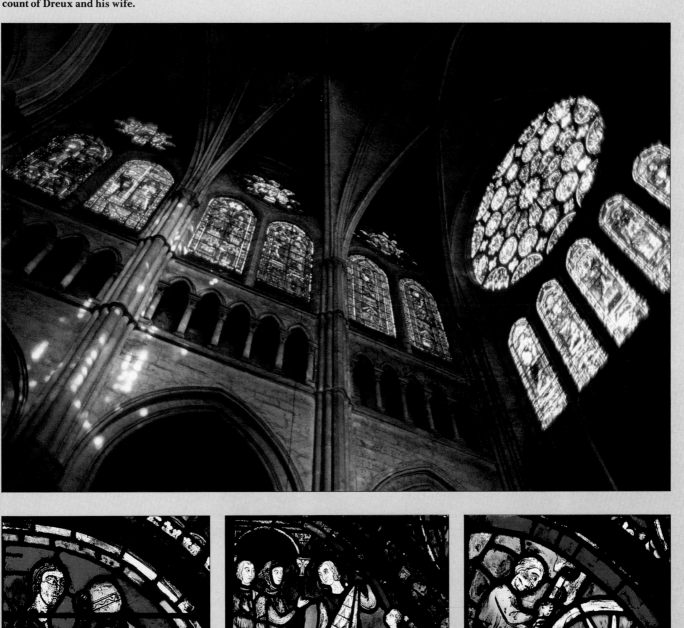

A water carrier pours out his wares.

A furrier sells a cloak.

A wheelwright plies his trade.

2

on the left bank of the Seine and commanding the burgesses to do likewise on the right bank.

His son and grandson, Louis VIII and Louis IX, conquered most of Languedoc and the county of Poitou. Champagne and Lyon were added by Philip IV (the "Fair") two generations later. But when the Valois — a younger branch of the Capetian dynasty — came to the throne in the 14th Century, the English kings pressed a rival claim to the French crown, based on descent through the female line.

During the Hundred Years' War that followed, from 1337 to 1453, the Eng-

lish won most of the battles. Yet just as the French cause seemed to be lost, a 17-year-old peasant girl came to rally the defenders. Joan of Arc could neither read nor write, but she had had visions and heard the voices of saints. Having persuaded the heir to the throne of her divine mission, she set off, on horseback and clothed in chain-mail, to lead an army of several thousand to the relief of Orléans. The English were forced to lift their siege and retreat beyond the Loire.

It was thanks to Joan that the young Charles VII was crowned King of France in Reims Cathedral on July 17,

1429. A year later, however, she was taken prisoner by the Burgundian allies of the English and turned over to a court at Rouen to be tried for heresy and witchcraft. Among the charges brought against her was that she had "put off the habit and dress of the female sex (which is contrary to divine law, abominable to God, condemned and prohibited by every law)" and had "dressed and armed herself in the state and habit of man." The judges were partisans of the English and the verdict was a foregone conclusion: Joan was burned at the stake on May 30, 1431. Her martyrdom, however, marked the

turning point of the Hundred Years' War. In French eyes this extraordinary woman in armor came to symbolize the spirit of patriotism and devotion that enabled the French kings to become masters in their own house.

Within 15 years of Joan's death, Charles had recruited the first royal army of France, consisting of 15 companies of noblemen volunteers, on horseback, to which he added a large body of conscript infantry and an artil-

lery section that proved to be the deadliest in Europe. French taxes had to be raised to foot the bill, but there was little doubt about the value of the investment after the last of the English armies was driven from France in 1453.

The long-awaited peace was marred by an ongoing rivalry between France and Burgundy — an issue that was finally settled when Louis XI annexed the duchy, together with Picardy, in 1477 after the death of its ruler Charles

the Bold. Brittany, Anjou and Provence, moreover, came to the French crown peacefully at this period, by marriage or bequest. The kingdom inherited by Francis I in 1515 was politically and culturally the largest unified state on the continent of Europe. Its frontiers were almost those of modern France, and the king's authority was now recognized by all of his great nobles. In governing the realm, Francis had the assistance of an increasing

49

SOUVENIRS OF THE REVOLUTION

Painted fan

Model guillotine

Sèvres urn with Liberty figure

Hardly any aspect of French life remained untouched by the social and political upheavals that followed the Revolution in 1789. Even the Gregorian calendar was abandoned for a rational system of seasonally named months, each 30 days; and a law removing restrictions in naming children produced such eccentricities as Mort aux Aristocrates ("Death to Aristocrats") or Racine de la Liberté ("Root of Liberty").

Just how far revolutionary zeal permeated everyday life is shown by the trinkets here, all of which promote revolutionary ideals. The fan and urn are decorated with the figure of Liberty bearing a spear surmounted by a red bonnet. Modeled on the headgear given to Roman slaves when they received their freedom, the "liberty cap" was a potent symbol of deliverance from repression. As such, it also forms the cover of a radical's inkwell *(opposite page, below left)*, where it symbolizes the crushing of the clergy by the forces of revolution.

Slogans promising "War to the Châteaux" and "Death to Tyrants" are inscribed on the snuffbox next to it, dedicated to the "brave sans-culottes of Paris" — the working people who wore long trousers rather than the knee breeches popular among the bourgeoisie. Similar sentiments hail from a pack of republican playing cards *(opposite, top right)* which, abandoning kings and queens as symbols of a past tyranny, bears representations of the ideals of the revolution. Among those shown are freedom of religion, racial equality and equal rights before the law.

Grim memories of the ancient regime are stirred by a barometer with a headpiece in the form of the Bastille — the infamous prison that symbolized royalist injustice. But the revolution in its turn was to spawn repression, commemorated here by a more sinister model guillotine of wood and cast iron.

Barometer with Bastille headpiece

Revolutionary playing cards

Liberty cap inkwell

Republican snuffbox

2

number of professional advisers — men from the middle classes specializing in law, taxation and finance, who were the forerunners of the army of bureaucrats that runs France today.

One of Francis' accomplishments was to bring the Italian Renaissance to his court. He collected Italian armor, employed Italian architects as well as painters — notably Leonardo da Vinci, who brought the *Mona Lisa* with him when he came to France — and commissioned Benvenuto Cellini to make statues for his increasingly Italianate palaces. His rivalry with the Hapsburg Emperor Charles V, later his brother-in-law, led to his capture and imprisonment; but after Francis had regained his freedom, he led an even more sumptuous life as a great collector of art and lover of beautiful women — a style that would be emulated by many of his successors.

The kings who followed him, however, were forced to deal with a new kind of political crisis. The Renaissance had ushered in a spirit of dissent and inquiry in religious and intellectual affairs, and these new currents culminated in the great schism known as the Reformation. France, like Germany, was split into warring camps of Catholics and Protestants, the latter were called Huguenots in France. After nearly 40 years of bitter, bloody civil war that devastated some of the nation's wealthiest cities, the rival parties compromised. They all united behind Henry IV, the first of the Bourbon branch of the French royal family to inherit the throne; he succeeded his heirless Valois cousin, Henry III, in 1589.

The fact that Henry had been educated as a Protestant at first seemed to exclude him from the succession, but after a timely conversion to Catholi-

cism — "Paris," he is alleged to have said, "is worth a mass" — he brought peace and prosperity to a war-weary people. He was an immensely popular monarch, "the only king remembered by the poor," largely because of his efforts to encourage French industry and agriculture: silk manufacturing, the weaving of Gobelin tapestries, the construction of canals, and much else besides. He was remembered, too, as a prodigious eater and drinker, and the sire of numerous children, legitimate and otherwise. He was assassinated in 1610 by a religious fanatic, but he had set France on a stable political course that enabled the first modern nation-state to weather the political storms that were to dismember Germany during the next half century.

His son, Louis XIII, upheld French unity in spite of renewed challenges from the Huguenots and other rebellious factions. A cautious, melancholy

monarch, he left the matter of government to his brilliant and much-hated first minister, Cardinal Richelieu, who proved to be far more able, and no less ruthless, than the high-placed nobles forever plotting his downfall.

Among Richelieu's most significant and long-term achievements was the creation of a navy. At the time of his rise to power in 1624, France had an insignificant force of armed ships, but two years later Richelieu appointed himself Superintendent of Navigation and Commerce and personally set about rectifying the situation, partly by buying boats from the Dutch. In addition, he encouraged overseas expansion, already begun in the 16th Century, by setting up a Marine Council to supervise it.

The vehicles of colonial growth were private companies operating under a royal charter, building settlements in far-flung lands to channel trade for their ships. In the years after Richelieu's death, governments did little to stimulate additional posts. Yet by the time that Colbert, the mercantilist minister of Louis XIII's son, the great Louis XIV, took up and developed the policies that Richelieu had set out, France already had interests in regions as far apart as Canada and the East Indies, Madagascar and the spice islands of the Caribbean, among them Guadeloupe and Martinique.

Louis XIV's reign began inauspiciously. The boy was only four years old in 1643 when his father died of tuberculosis, and soon many of the leading nobles were in open revolt against the crown. For the next 10 years, France was ruled by a regency in which Richelieu's successor, Cardinal Mazarin, exercised considerable powers. During civil disturbances in 1651, a mob con-

Wearing his imperial uniform, Napoleon Bonaparte stands in a characteristic pose for a portrait by Jacques-Louis David, appointed court painter at Napoleon's coronation. The lives of both, subject and painter, ended miserably, in exile.

verged on the Palais Royal in Paris,
hammered on the doors and demanded to see the king — there were rumors
that he had left the capital. The 12-
year-old Louis had to pretend to be
asleep while a delegation filed past the
royal bed to be reassured that he was
still in residence. The lesson was not
lost on Louis, who was to move the seat
of government to Versailles — then a
day's ride from the city — where he
could rule the nation undisturbed by
the mutinous and perpetually threatening rabble of Paris.

The great palace built at Versailles
was Louis XIV's personal concept and
creation. He inherited its nucleus — a
royal hunting lodge set in an unprepos-
sessing landscape. With the help of the
finest architects, sculptors and landscape gardeners of the realm, and the
expenditure of 65 million *livres* (at a
time when an ordinary house cost
about 20 *livres* to construct), he turned
Versailles into the most magnificent
royal residence in the whole of Europe.
Its stately galleries and vast hall of mir-
rors, its spacious boudoirs and orna-
mental gardens, were the outward
manifestations of France's prosperity
and the king's unprecedented power.

But Versailles also represented a
means of depriving the great nobles of
the last vestiges of their independence.
Many of the dukes and counts who had
once been autonomous in their impreg-
nable castles were now reduced to the
status of courtiers at Versailles. They
spent their lives participating in the
elaborate ritual of the king's comings
and goings, dancing in the gorgeously
costumed court ballets — Louis himself
used to dance the role of *le Roi Soleil*, the
Sun King — and riding in the horseback pageants known as *carrousels*. To
others, however, it seemed that the
worst fate that could befall them was to
be banished from this dazzling palace,
the home of all civilized pleasures and
comforts, and to be exiled to the tedium
of a provincial château.

Louis's 72-year reign represented
the apogee of French power and prestige in monarchical Europe. During
that time the rest of the world came to
look on France as the arbiter of fashion
in dress, architecture, furniture and
the decorative arts; throughout Europe, kings and princes were building
their own reduced-scale copies of Versailles. But Louis also had dreams of
military glory, and he undertook to enlarge his domains still further, in Flanders and Alsace-Lorraine, and it was
these wars of conquest rather than his
construction projects that depleted the
royal treasury. He grew so old that he
outlived his son the Dauphin (as the
crown princes of France were known)
and also the Dauphin's son, and was
succeeded in 1715 by his five-year-old
great-grandson, Louis XV.

The nation was ruled by a regent,
Philippe d'Orléans, but even after
Louis XV had attained his majority, he
entrusted the government to his ministers and devoted himself to the pursuit
of happiness at Versailles and the company of his *maîtresse en titre* (the officially recognized mistress), Madame de
Pompadour. She owed her power over
the king as much to her intelligence and
taste as to her radiant good looks. She
alone knew how to keep him amused,
by staging private theatricals and com-
missioning paintings, sculptures and
palaces. But she also befriended and
encouraged such writers as Voltaire,
Diderot and d'Alembert — the philo-
sophically minded authors who were
ushering in the Age of Enlightenment,
and whose work pointed the way to ra-

30,000-15,000 B.C. Cro-Magnon man, the first ancestor of today's *homo sapiens,* populates a France emptied by the Ice Age. These Stone Age hunters paint animals on the walls of the caves in which they live *(above).*

4,000-2,000 B.C. Tribes of the New Stone Age, growing grain and raising domestic animals, inhabit most of the area of modern-day France. They leave behind them the stone monuments known as menhirs and dolmens.

800-400 B.C. Celtic tribes — later known to the Romans as Gauls — invade from across the Rhine and divide the territory of France into many small states.

c.600 B.C. Greek traders found the city of Massilia — now Marseille — on the Mediterranean coast.

387 B.C. Celts invade Italy and sack Rome.

121 B.C. The Romans annex the area bordering the Mediterranean now known as Provence.

58-50 B.C. Rome declares war on the Gauls. In an eight-year campaign, Julius Caesar conquers the whole of present-day France and adjacent territories as far as the Rhine. Vercingetorix, the Gallic leader, is captured and taken prisoner to Rome.

50 B.C.-406 A.D. The victorious Romans establish a unified administration, centered on their capital Lugdunum (now Lyon). Gallo-Roman civilization flourishes during a prolonged period of peace *(right).*

313 By the Edict of Milan, the Emperor Constantine proclaims liberty of conscience throughout the Roman Empire. Christianity spreads rapidly in Gaul.

406-450 The Romans withdraw their garrisons from the Rhine frontier. Waves of invaders — Franks, Burgundians, Vandals, Visigoths — sweep into the country from the east.

451 The Huns led by Attila, invade Gaul. They are driven back in the battle of Moirey.

481-511 Clovis becomes king of the Franks, who have settled in northeastern Gaul. In the course of his reign he defeats the Gallo-Romans, Burgundians and Visigoths, and establishes Frankish control over the whole of France. Baptized in 496, he becomes the first Christian king of France. His successors found the Merovingian dynasty.

732 Charles Martel drives back Muslims invading France from Spain at the battle of Poitiers.

751 Pepin, mayor of the palace, deposes the last Merovingian king, Childeric III, and takes the throne, founding the Carolingian dynasty.

800 Coronation of the Carolingian king Charlemagne — Charles the Great — as emperor of a domain incorporating France, Germany, northern Italy, and northeastern Spain.

843 Charlemagne's empire is divided among his grandsons. France falls to Charles the Bald.

877-987 On the death of Charles the Bald, the decline of central power accelerates, leaving France as a loose collection of feudal lordships owing at most a nominal allegiance to the king.

911 Viking invaders are granted the northwestern lands around the river Seine that become the Duchy of Normandy. Its Norman rulers conquer England after winning the Battle of Hastings in 1066 *(below).*

987 Hugh Capet, Count of Paris, is elected king of France, with only nominal power over his fellow nobles who elected him. Over the next three centuries his descendants, of the Capetian dynasty, gradually reassert and expand the power of the monarchy over the feudal lords.

1194-1260 Chartres Cathedral, the purest example of French Gothic architecture, is built.

1207-1223 King Philip Augustus leads a crusade against the Albigensian heretics of southern France. After a long and bitter campaign, he succeeds in annexing Languedoc and crushes the heretics with a bloody repression.

1214 Philip Augustus defeats the English at the battle of Bouvines, and wins Normandy and other English possessions on the continent.

1226-1270 Reign of Louis IX, the greatest of Capetian kings. His reputation extends throughout Europe, and in 1297 he is posthumously canonized for his part in organizing the Seventh Crusade.

1309-1377 To escape factionalism in

Rome, Pope Clement V moves the seat of the Papacy to Avignon. In all, seven successive French Popes rule the Church from the city for 68 years.

1328 The Capetian dynasty becomes extinct on the death of Charles IV. He is succeeded by Philip VI, founder of the Valois dynasty that rules France until the late 16th Century.

1337 Rival claims of the English King Edward III to the throne of the Valois lead to the outbreak of the Hundred Years' War between England and France.

1348-1350 The Black Death — an outbreak of bubonic plague — ravages France and much of the rest of Europe, killing up to one third of the entire population of the country.

c.1410 The *Très Riches Heures du Duc de Berry,* greatest of illuminated manuscripts, is painted by the Limbourg brothers for a brother of Charles V.

1415 French forces suffer a major defeat at the hands of the English longbowmen at the battle of Agincourt.

1429 Joan of Arc relieves Orléans, besieged by the English. She inspires a national revival under the young King Charles VII before she is captured, handed over to the English and burned at the stake in 1431.

1453 Battle of Castillon marks the end of the Hundred Years' War. The English lose all their possessions in France except Calais, finally regained by the French 105 years later.

1461-1483 Reign of Louis XI, whose ruthless dedication to the task of expanding royal authority leads to the development of centralized power at the expense of the feudal nobility.

1515-1547 Reign of Francis I, whose rule marks the full flowering of the Renaissance in France.

1532 Brittany is formally incorporated into France by marriage. The liberties of the province are guaranteed, and it retains its autonomy until 1790.

1532-35 François Rabelais writes *Gargantua and Pantagruel,* whose satirical assaults on established religion and conventional wisdom typify the questioning spirit of the Renaissance.

1562-1598 Wars of Religion set the Catholics against the Protestant Huguenots.

1572 St. Bartholomew's Day massacre: thousands of Huguenots killed.

1589 Henry III, the last Valois king of France, dies childless. He is succeeded by Henry IV, founder of the Bourbon dynasty *(below).*

1598 Edict of Nantes: Henry IV grants toleration of Protestant religion.

1624-1642 Louis XIII appoints Cardinal Richelieu as his chief minister. For the next 18 years until his death, Richelieu works ceaselessly to maintain royal power and authority.

1637 René Descartes publishes his *Discourse on Method* — the classic statement of French rationalism.

1643-1715 Reign of Louis XIV, the Sun King, marks the apogee of absolute monarchy.

1685 Louis XIV revokes the Edict of Nantes, leading to large-scale Huguenot emigration.

1715 Louis XV accedes to the throne, inheriting a country rich in prestige but financially exhausted by the Sun King's continual wars. The pleasure-loving monarch devotes more time to his mistresses, of whom the most influential is Mme de Pompadour *(above),* than to affairs of state; military reversals in the Seven Years' War with England (1756-63) and financial mismanagement combine to weaken royal authority. In the arts, the exuberant Rococo style flourishes.

1756 Publication of the first volume of the *Encyclopédie,* edited by Denis Diderot, and aimed to advance "reason, knowledge and liberty." With Voltaire, the "Encyclopedists" are the standard-bearers of the Age of Reason, combating obscurantism and religious intolerance.

1762 Rousseau publishes *The Social Contract,* which argues that man was created free and equal and that society has created inequality and misery.

1774 Louis XVI succeeds Louis XV as ruler of France.

1782 The Montgolfier brothers conduct the first hot-air balloon ascents, at first unmanned and the next year with human passengers *(above)*, ushering in the era of manned flight.

1789 Meeting of the Estates-General marks the start of the French Revolution. A mob of Parisians storms the Bastille, a prison fortress that has become a symbol of monarchical repression.

1792 Louis XVI is deposed, to be tried and executed the following year *(below)*. France is declared a republic.

1799 Napoleon Bonaparte is appointed First Consul of France.

1804 Napoleon is made Emperor. The First Empire succeeds the First Republic.

1812 Napoleon's empire reaches its greatest extent when Russia is invaded; but the campaign ends in disaster when the French Army is forced to retreat from Moscow two months later.

1814 Forced to abdicate, Napoleon is exiled to Elba. The Bourbons are restored to the throne, with limited powers, in the person of Louis XVIII, brother of Louis XVI.

1815 Napoleon escapes and raises a new army. Defeated at the Battle of Waterloo, he is sent into final exile to the South Atlantic island of St. Helena.

1824 Charles X succeeds Louis XVIII.

1830 The July Revolution: Charles abdicates and is replaced by Louis Philippe, heir to the Orléans branch of the Bourbon dynasty and a supporter of constitutional monarchy.

1830-1847 Algeria is conquered by French colonial forces.

1833 Marie-Antoine Carême, the codifier of classic French cookery, publishes *The Art of Cooking in the 19th Century*, a compendium of *haute cuisine*.

1848 Following the Revolution of 1848, Louis Philippe is overthrown and the Second Republic is established, under the presidency of Bonaparte's nephew Louis-Napoleon — caricatured below in later life.

1851 Louis-Napoleon stages a *coup d'état*, dissolving the assembly and promising a new constitution. The following year, he is elected Emperor as Napoleon III, and the Second Republic gives way to the Second Empire.

1853-1870 As prefect of Paris, Baron Georges-Eugène Haussmann organizes a massive rebuilding program, modernizing the capital's transport and sanitation facilities and constructing the Opera, the Les Halles market complex and the *grands boulevards*.

1860 By the Treaty of Turin, Nice and Savoy are ceded to France by the Kingdom of Sardinia in return for French support for Italian reunification.

1861 Louis Pasteur develops the germ theory of disease, which he subsequently applies in developing the pasteurization process for sterilizing liquids.

1870 The Prussians invade France and, after the Battle of Sedan, force Napoleon III to capitulate. The Second Empire falls, and the Third Republic is proclaimed.

1871 France cedes Alsace and Lorraine to Prussia. Revolutionaries seize control of Paris and declare it a commune, only to be bloodily suppressed by government troops.

1872 Claude Monet paints *Impression Sunrise,* the canvas that later gives its name to the Impressionist movement.

1875-1887 Phylloxera epidemic ravages one third of France's vineyards. The destruction is ultimately halted by grafting native vines onto roots imported from the United States that are resistant to the pest.

1890-1914 The *belle époque* — a stable era of good living — marks life, especially in Paris, before World War I *(above).* It was a period of considerable artistic activity that saw the flowering of the Art Nouveau style of sinuous and elaborate design.

1894 Colonel Alfred Dreyfus is convicted by court martial of selling secrets to the Germans. The Dreyfus affair splits the nation, half believing him guilty, others protesting his innocence.

1903 Pierre and Marie Curie share the Nobel Prize for Physics with Becquerel for the discovery of radioactivity.

1909 Louis Blériot becomes the first man to fly in a heavier-than-air craft across the English Channel.

1914 World War I begins.

1918 France emerges from the War victorious but exhausted, with much of her industry ruined and nearly 1.4 million men dead.

1919 By the Treaty of Versailles, France regains Alsace and Lorraine.

1925 The Exposition des Arts Décoratifs is held in Paris, giving its name to the modernist style of decoration known as Art Deco.

1936 The parties of the left come to power as the Popular Front, under the Socialist Léon Blum.

1939 World War II begins.

1940 France surrenders to Germany. The Third Republic ends, and the collaborationist Vichy government of Marshal Pétain governs France.

1944 Allied forces liberate France *(below).* General de Gaulle, head of the Free French Forces, becomes head of a provisional government.

1946 The Fourth Republic is established.

1946-1955 Le Corbusier, France's most celebrated 20th Century architect, creates his best-known French works — the *unité d'habitation* (living unit), a high-rise development in Marseille, and the chapel of Notre-Dame-du-Haut at Ronchamp in Franche-Comté.

1947 Christian Dior creates a fashion sensation with his "New Look" *(above).*

1949 France joins the North Atlantic Treaty Organization (NATO).

1954 The fall of Dien Bien Phu leads to French withdrawal from Vietnam.

1958 An insurrection by French forces in Algeria leads to the collapse of the Fourth Republic. General de Gaulle returns to power, and the Fifth Republic is established.

1960 France explodes its first atomic bomb.

1962 France agrees to withdraw from Algeria. Algerian independence is proclaimed.

1966 France withdraws from military commitments to NATO.

1968 A wave of student riots and strikes signals popular discontent with de Gaulle's rule. A reaction to the disorders then sets in, and later in the year voters return the Gaullists to power with an increased majority.

1969 De Gaulle resigns. He is succeeded as President by Georges Pompidou.

1974 Valéry Giscard d'Estaing becomes President on the death of Pompidou.

1981 The Socialist François Mitterrand is elected President. The Left sweeps to victory in parliamentary elections. The new Council of Ministers includes four Communists.

1984 The Communist Party walks out of Mitterrand's Socialist government.

2

tionalism and, ultimately, revolution.

During the 18th Century, the French economy came to depend increasingly on trade between metropolitan France and her colonies in the West Indies, whose slave-produced sugar, coffee and spices were processed at Bordeaux, Nantes and Rochefort before being re-exported to other European markets. Rival French and British mercantile interests led repeatedly to war on the high seas, in which the British fleet regularly outnumbered and outgunned

the French navy. While Louis XV dallied at Versailles, his generals and their armies continued to dominate Western Europe, but his admirals lost the war at sea. Eventually, France was forced to relinquish her Indian colonies as well as her Canadian possessions and most of her Caribbean islands.

Not until the 1760s did France begin to build a navy commensurate with her far-flung overseas interests. The opportunity to use the powerful new ships of the line came in 1776, two years after

the young Louis XVI had succeeded to the throne. Great Britain's American colonies had declared their independence, and during the Revolutionary War that followed, the French fleet under Admiral de Grasse cooperated with General Washington's army to bring about the surrender of the British expeditionary force at Yorktown, Virginia. The 1783 treaty that was negotiated in Paris between representatives of Great Britain and of the American Congress (which included Benjamin

Franklin and Thomas Jefferson) brought an end to the American Revolution and accomplished formal recognition of the United States as an independent power.

But the triumph of democratic principles — many of them borrowed from the French thinkers of the Enlightenment — in the new American republic was to create a dangerous political precedent. Already there was no lack of voices in France advocating the doctrine of sovereignty of the people, and calling for abolition of the hereditary privileges of the nobility, among them exemption from paying taxes. At the same time, the costs of the war and a series of financial disasters brought the nation to the verge of bankruptcy. In 1789, the Estates-General — a special assembly which had last convened in 1614 — met to try and resolve the crisis. When the assembly began its deliberations, the representatives of the Third Estate — the house representing those who were neither nobles nor churchmen — refused to do the government's bidding and declared themselves the sovereign power of France.

The first revolution in the defiant National Assembly was followed by a second in the streets of Paris. On July 14, 1789, an angry mob stormed the Bastille, the hated royal prison on the right bank of the Seine, and carried off the governor's head on a pike. About three months later, another mob, led by the fishwives of Paris, converged on Versailles and brought Louis XVI and his family to live as virtual prisoners in the Tuileries, a half-abandoned wing of the Louvre. In June 1791, the royal family escaped from the palace by night, were caught at Varennes 17 miles away, and taken back to Paris by a roundabout, four-day route intended to exhibit the unhappy royal captives to the common people. Louis, a harmless man who had dreamed of establishing charities for the poor, was eventually tried and convicted of having "conspired against the liberty of the nation." He went to the guillotine in January 1793 — as "Citizen Capet." Nine months later Marie-Antoinette, his wife, suffered the same fate.

Meanwhile, the French Revolution gathered momentum. A succession of popular assemblies decreed sweeping changes in the structure and function of the new government. The clergy and aristocracy lost their privileges; lands belonging to the Catholic Church — about 20 per cent of the total area of France — were confiscated. The "rights of man" were written in a new constitution and the judiciary and defense establishments were overhauled. For a time, France adopted a revolutionary calendar, ostensibly more scientific than the Gregorian one, which divided the year into months with such rationalist names as *Nivôse* ("the snowy month"), *Germinal* ("seed time") and *Thermidor* ("the warm month").

It was not long before the revolutionary government was forced to defend its frontiers against monarchist armies pouring across the Rhine River. At Valmy, on September 20, 1792, a force of 50,000 French soldiers fighting for "Liberty, Equality, Fraternity," the watchwords of the Revolution, defeated an army of 80,000 Germans and others who had been sent to reinstate the old order. The poet Johann Wolfgang von Goethe, who had accompanied the German troops, immediately recognized the historic significance of the fighting he had just witnessed. "From this place and from this day forward commences a new era in the world's his-tory," he told the German officers, "and you can all say that you were present at its birth."

After the proclamation of the Republic on September 22, 1792, the leadership of the Revolution passed from the moderates to the radicals under Robespierre, the "incorruptible" dictator who sent thousands of his adversaries to the guillotine. Not until Robespierre himself was executed on the 10th of Thermidor (July 28), 1794, did the Reign of Terror come to an end and the country regain a measure of political equilibrium.

The government, a five-man Directory, entrusted its defense to a brilliant young Corsican artillery officer, Napoleon Bonaparte, who had proved his mettle by quelling a street demonstration with what was later described in a celebrated phrase as a "whiff of grapeshot." As a field commander he knew better than anyone else how to mobilize the revolutionary ardor of his hungry and ragged soldiers. In 1795, he made short work of the Austrians in northern Italy, reequipped his men with the captured material, and remitted enormous sums of money to replenish the depleted French treasury.

It was only a matter of time before this ruthlessly energetic general took over the government — initially, after a coup d'état in 1799, as "First Consul," then "Emperor of the French." Within a decade, Napoleon's armies had extended the French imperium from the Iberian peninsula to the Neva River. But although he tried to legitimize his position by divorcing his first wife and marrying Marie Louise, a daughter of the Austrian emperor, his autocratic regime was propped up solely by the bayonets of his grenadiers.

After years of victories, he finally

In the Place Vendôme, supporters of the 1871 Paris Commune pose by a fallen statue of Napoleon I dressed in imperial Roman garb. The monument was toppled on the orders of left-wing communards, for whom it signified autocracy and repression.

outreached himself and encountered a series of disasters. His abortive invasion of Russia in 1812 cost him half a million men, and there were other defeats in Spain and Leipzig. Forced to abdicate, he was sent to the tiny Italian island of Elba, where it was hoped that he would live out the remainder of his life as a kind of comic-opera monarch. Instead he escaped and embarked on the desperate comeback attempt now known as the Hundred Days, only to see his last hopes extinguished at the Battle of Waterloo on June 18, 1815. This time the British shipped him off to St. Helena, in the South Atlantic, from which there was no returning.

Napoleon's downfall was to be followed by the restoration of the monarchy. Louis XVI's brother, the Count of Provence, emerged from exile in England to be crowned Louis XVIII (his nephew, the Dauphin, who had died in prison, was considered to have been Louis XVII after his father's execution). The returned nobles made tentative efforts to reassert their privileges, but it was the middle classes who prevailed over the old regime and retained their parliamentary influence and the other rights they had won during the Revolution. After the death of Louis XVIII — the last king of France to die while still a reigning monarch — the throne passed to his brother, who was crowned Charles X at Reims in 1825 with all the traditional pomp and pageantry. Charles tried to come to terms with the liberal and radical factions that vied for control of the Chamber of Deputies, but his ill-timed attempt to control the parliament and censor the press provoked yet another insurrection in the streets of Paris — the July Revolution of 1830.

This time, however, the uprising was not followed by scenes of terror and the tumbling of eminent heads into waiting baskets. Although there was talk of restoring the Republic of 1793, the Revolution was quietly sidetracked by the nervous leaders of the moderate center, who offered the crown of France to Louis Philippe, Duke of Orléans, a cousin of the deposed king.

For 18 years, the self-styled "citizen king" managed to keep a semblance of harmony among the bitter rivals contending for power in the legislature. It was a time of growing commercial and industrial prosperity — and against this background of bourgeois affluence the artists and the writers of France created a French flowering of the Europe-wide revolution in sensibility known as the Romantic movement.

Romanticism in France consisted of Victor Hugo's writings and Hector Berlioz' symphonies; the paintings of Eugène Delacroix and the novels of Honoré de Balzac and George Sand; the nocturnes of Polish-born Frédéric Chopin, who spent much of his life in France, the poetry of Alfred de Musset and Gérard de Nerval. Yet mounting discontent among the workers, and the grinding poverty that Hugo described in his epic novel *Les Misérables,* erupted in the February Revolution of 1848. The last king of France fled to England; now there was to be a republic on the American model, headed by a president with executive powers.

At the first presidential election, the front runner was Louis-Napoleon Bonaparte, a nephew of the great emperor. Buoyed by the enduring popular nostalgia for his uncle's empire, he won a landslide victory. Two years later he, too, swept aside the inconveniences of parliamentary democracy and took the name and style of Emperor Napoleon

Built for the Great Exhibition of 1889 to symbolize technological progress, the half-finished Eiffel Tower takes on its now world-famous form. Designed by Alexandre Gustave Eiffel, the edifice was condemned as a monstrosity by most commentators at the time. The public loved it.

III. (Napoleon's son, the Duke of Reichstadt, who had died in 1832, was held to have been "Napoleon II.")

The two decades of the Second Empire were to coincide with an unprecedented expansion of business and industry. The population of Paris, just over half a million in 1801, reached nearly two million by 1866. Yet the new emperor — whom Victor Hugo had sized up as "Napoleon the Little" — wanted more than domestic affluence. He had grandiose international ambitions and became embroiled with Italy, Russia, Austria and even Mexico. During the summer of 1870, Prussia's Otto von Bismarck, who had done more than any other man to unite the German nation, maneuvered the emperor into a war for which France was manifestly unprepared. Less than seven weeks after the outbreak of hostilities, the bulk of the French army, led by the emperor himself, capitulated to the Prussians at Sedan.

The political leaders of Paris reacted to the news by proclaiming a provincial government. Because the republic refused to cede the provinces of Alsace and Lorraine to Prussia, the invading army surrounded the city and mounted a siege from September 19 to January 28, when the French at last agreed to pay a heavy indemnity and surrender the disputed territory. The government of the Third Republic was a provisional coalition dominated by conservative elements. When its officials tried to remove some of the artillery belonging to the Paris militia, the workers rose in revolt and formed their own radical government, the Commune.

For two months, the Commune held out against a second siege of Paris, this time conducted by French troops loyal to the central government. There were

In Jean Béraud's *The Night Moths*, painted in 1905, shimmering ladies promenade past bourgeois gentlemen in a lamplit garden scene that epitomizes the opulence of France's *belle époque*, or "beautiful era" — a time of wealth and optimism cut short by the cataclysm of World War I.

2

French reservists stream out of Paris' Gare du Nord after enlisting at the outbreak of World War I in 1914. At war's end France won back Alsace and Lorraine, lost to Germany in the Franco-Prussian War almost 50 years earlier. But the cost — more than a million dead — was terrible.

atrocities on both sides, and when the besiegers finally stormed the city in May 1871, they shot thousands of the Communard prisoners out of hand.

The scars left by this terrible year seemed almost beyond healing, yet in fact the process of reconstruction got under way almost immediately. By 1878, the year of the Universal Exhibition, a British journalist could write a book entitled *Paris Herself Again,* noting that the city had become "comelier, richer, gayer, more fascinating than ever." What had transpired since the war's end was nothing less than an economic miracle. "Defeated France has risen to its feet," wrote Émile Zola, the novelist-reporter of the epoch, "and has triumphed in art and industry."

Indeed, during the 40 years between the Franco-Prussian War and World War I, France regained not only its prosperity but its preeminence in arts and letters. In painting, the Impressionists and Post-Impressionists used sunlight and vivid color to demolish the tedium of official art. A similar development took place in the world of music, in the luminescent tones of composers like Camille Saint-Saëns, Claude Debussy and Maurice Ravel. Auguste Rodin's *The Thinker* and *The Kiss* established new precedents in sculpture. French literature flourished and became a booming industry. If a novel by Zola "does not sell three hundred thousand copies it is a failure," marveled the Anglo-Irish writer George Moore. "Did any great writer ever see literature from this point of view before?" But there was a market, too, for the esoteric but influential poetry of the likes of Paul Verlaine and Stéphane Mallarmé.

The *belle époque* (literally "beautiful era") of the 1890s seemed to herald a new century that would be suffused

with the spirit of humanism and of idealism. For the first time in history the intellectual aristocracy replaced the landed nobility as the most influential class in France. Then, almost without warning, World War I descended on Europe like a giant guillotine. In four years of fighting against the invading German army, from 1914 to 1918, France lost nearly 1.4 million men. In 1916, the Battle of Verdun alone cost France more than 150,000 men.

When the Germans surrendered, France recovered Alsace and Lorraine and was awarded enormous financial reparations. It was the long-awaited revenge for the defeat of 1871. But the cycle of retaliation did not end there. In retrospect the 1920s and '30s were little more than a breathing space in what the poet-diplomat Paul Claudel

was to call the "Thirty Years' War."

Internally, the Third Republic was in its decadence. The divisions already existing in French politics had been heightened by the Russian Revolution of 1917, which had led to a split in the Socialist Party; in 1920, a pro-Russian wing broke away to form the French Communist Party. On the right, the fear of Bolshevism encouraged semifascist groups such as the militantly royalist Action Française.

Between these extremes, the republic struggled to survive and move forward under the indecisive leadership of a succession of coalition governments. Already politically weak, France was then stricken, like the rest of the Western industrialized world, by the economic depression of the '30s. The nation was swept by social unrest, and for

A swastika flies from the Arc de Triomphe after the German occupation of Paris in 1940. Most Parisians went to such lengths to avoid contact with the 30,000-strong occupying forces that they earned the capital the nickname "the city that never looks at you."

a time the danger of civil breakdown seemed real. In 1936, the parties of the left came together in face of the danger of a right-wing coup to form the Popular Front, which came to power in the elections of May of that year. In its two years in office, the Popular Front introduced such reforms as paid holidays for workers and a 40-hour work week. In 1938, when it fell from power, France was still dangerously divided, and was also threatened externally by a ring of hostile dictatorships around her borders: Hitler in Germany, Mussolini in Italy, Franco in Spain.

When World War II broke out the following year, France at first seemed safe behind the carefully prepared fortifications of the Maginot Line, a belt of concrete bunkers and tank traps strung out along the whole of her frontier with Germany. But Hitler chose to attack France through the neutral countries of Belgium and Luxembourg, where the borders were relatively undefended. In the spring of 1940, the German *Blitzkrieg* rolled across northern France. Paris was declared an open city and offered no resistance. By June 14, the swastikas were flying over the Crillon Hotel, where the German military governor set up his temporary headquarters. The invaders came from the direction of Saint-Denis and the northeastern suburbs. "First motorcyclists with sidecars, in their leather overcoats," the Paris Chief of Police Roger Langeron noted in his diary. "Then the weight of the armor, of tanks. The streets are virtually empty, and the majority of houses are shuttered."

France capitulated. Marshal Pétain, an aging hero of World War I, assumed dictatorial powers as the chief of state, removing the word "republic" from official papers and replacing the motto

"Liberty, Equality, Fraternity" with the vapid "Work, Family, Fatherland." While the Germans settled into Paris and occupied northern France, the Pétain government took up residence at Vichy, formerly famous for its mineral springs, which became the provisional capital of the unoccupied zone. The line of demarcation between the two zones was to become an impenetrable barrier for all but a favored few. For four years, the Vichy government cooperated with Nazi authorities, helping them secure more than a million workers for German war industries and to round up thousands of Jews to be shipped to Nazi extermination camps.

At this unpropitious moment in the history of France, a man of destiny emerged on the scene. Charles de Gaulle was a career soldier, little known other than as the author of books on leadership and military matters, who had just been given a government post as undersecretary of state for defense and war when France capitulated. He escaped to England, establishing a Free French government in exile that gradually succeeded in rallying French resistance against Hitler, both within France and in the overseas colonies. It was a Free French division, that of General Jacques Philippe Leclerc, which was chosen to spearhead the liberation of Paris on August 24, 1944. Once again there was no real resistance; despite Hitler's order that the city was to be set on fire, the French capital was one of the few major cities within the orbit of the Third Reich to escape serious damage. One of the first acts of the new government was to nullify the laws and directives of the Vichy regime. There were writers who spoke of the war as "four years to strike from our history."

More important, the way was open

for the nation's escape from the nightmare of war and foreign occupation. In the moment of victory, the common patriotism forged a fragile unity. In practice, France remained divided; even the victorious Resistance was split between its major factions, Gaullists loyal to their wartime leader, and Communists, who had played a crucial role after the Germans invaded the U.S.S.R. in 1941. Yet these divisions were temporarily hidden under a common mantle of hope and the desire to begin anew.

The Liberation was a new dawn. In a referendum in 1945, an overwhelming 96 per cent of the population voted against the restoration of the old Third Republic. The nation wanted to start afresh, and it was ready for the hard work of construction. □

63

IMAGES OF THE RURAL PAST

Far into the present century, the pace of agricultural progress in France was slow. Until World War II, most farmers owned or rented properties smaller than 12 acres. Capital to acquire modern equipment was hard to find, and rural life retained a traditional character long left behind in neighboring Germany and Britain.

Times have changed since then, and much of modern French agriculture is prosperous, dynamic and efficient. Yet many people regret the passing of the old ways, despite the poverty that accompanied them. They cherish a past in which independently minded peasant families worked the land with their own hands, when horses and oxen still pulled the plows and wagons, and mechanization was limited to a seasonal visit from a communal threshing machine.

That vanished pastoral world is recorded with unsentimental respect in an unparalleled archive of photographs taken from 1912 onward at the behest of a far-sighted banker from Alsace. Albert Kahn was a self-made man who spent his enthusiasm and his wealth unstintingly on idealistic projects to foster international understanding, including the creation of a photographic record of the inhabited world as it was at the beginning of the 20th Century. France was only one of 38 countries covered by his teams of lensmen, using the newly developed "autochrome" process, an early form of color photography that produced a delicately tinted image on a glass plate.

Selected from the 72,000 pictures in the Kahn collection, now in the possession of the state, the views of rural France shown here were taken between 1916 and 1921. Most of the activities they capture, however, were still common sights at the end of World War II.

Beneath the imposing walls of the Gothic cathedral of St. Paul Aurélien, peasants in 1920 marshal their wagons for the daily cauliflower market in the Breton town of Saint-Pol-de-Léon. The cauliflowers — the district's main crop — were bought by wholesalers for distribution throughout France.

A couple prepares tiles for a method of oyster farming practiced in the bay of Arcachon, west of Bordeaux, from the 1860s to the present day. Coated with a sand-and-whitewash mix, the tiles were sunk in the bay to attract oyster larvae, which were later transferred to wire cages near the shore to mature.

At Esnandes near La Rochelle on the
west coast of France, a mussel farmer
pauses in the work of unloading his
crop, a profitable local trade since the
13th Century. The mollusks fixed
themselves to wooden stakes dug into
the sea bottom, and were gathered into
baskets from a boat at low tide.

Teams of heavy horses pull two-wheeled carts collecting bales of hay in a meadow west of Paris in the fertile Ile de France region. Shaped with the aid of a horse-drawn baler, bales were loaded by hand onto the carts and taken to a farm for indoor storage.

At Morvan in Burgundy in the summer of 1916, men and women toil side by side at the backbreaking task of gathering hay. The mowed grass was tossed for several days under the sun until it was dry, then raked and forked onto an ox-drawn wagon.

A farmer near Saint-Macaire in Aquitaine plows his field for spring sowing in 1921, using a team of oxen and a plow of a type that had changed little over the centuries. Oxen, though slow, made strong and reliable draft animals, and were less expensive to buy than horses.

In a vineyard west of Clermont-Ferrand in the Auvergne, a girl empties her grapes into a wicker basket of a traditional local pattern, carried by a boy who patrolled the rows of vines for the bunches cut by the women. The grapes were poured into wooden vats and taken by cart back to a farm.

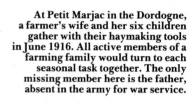

At Petit Marjac in the Dordogne, a farmer's wife and her six children gather with their haymaking tools in June 1916. All active members of a farming family would turn to each seasonal task together. The only missing member here is the father, absent in the army for war service.

Seated around a threshing machine at harvest time, workers in the Aquitaine region near the Pyrenees raise their glasses of wine in a toast. Drawn from village to village by a traction engine, the machine's arrival was a signal for communal festivity as well as a bout of hard work.

THE TRADITION OF CENTRALIZATION

A quorum of the 491 members of the National Assembly, France's main legislative body, await the President before the day's proceedings. The worldwide political use of "right" and "left" derives from the seating plan, with conservatives to the right of the rostrum, socialists opposite.

France has long been regarded as the most centralized nation in the West, with the government taking charge of many matters that in other lands are usually left to local bodies or to private enterprise. The average Frenchman sends his children to state schools, and if they go on to a university, it will be a state one too. When sick, he enters a state hospital. He travels on state railroads and airlines, and his car may well be the product of Renault, a state-owned company. He puts his money in a state bank, and he smokes cigarettes sold by the state tobacco monopoly; and in civic affairs, at least until recently, in order to build on his own land, or to start a sports or arts club, or to open a store, the permit would be granted to him not by the town council of his municipality but by the prefect — a powerful local government potentate who is appointed by and answerable to the state.

The many threads of this complex power network lead inexorably back to the hundreds of central offices in Paris where all, or nearly all, the important decisions of government are made. This degree of centralized control, common in the Communist world, is rare in a democratic, multiparty nation such as France, and the reasons for it must be sought far back in French history. Ever since the Capetian kings in the Middle Ages forged one nation out of the diverse peoples living in what is now France, the country's rulers have

struggled to maintain a centralized structure to prevent it from flying apart. The process was reinforced by the postrevolutionary rulers who, after 1789, devised a system of government that has persisted almost to this day, with Paris-appointed prefects ruling autocratically over the 90-odd departments into which the country is administratively divided.

The system of state control — it is called *étatisme*, or statism — has long been criticized by the French themselves. Many believe that the vigorous dominance of government-appointed technocrats breeds apathy among the ordinary people, and either stunts local initiative or else drives it into systematic opposition.

Administrations themselves have been aware of the problem, and since the last war have made some moves toward decentralization. The issue is annoying, however, for it could equally well be argued that *étatisme* has brought real advantages to France. It has facilitated economic planning. And in the years after the end of World War II in particular, the stability of the powerful civil service provided a healthy antidote to the instability of a sequence of short-lived governments.

France emerged from the war sickened by the decadence of the Third Republic and determined to make a fresh start; so in 1946 the Fourth Republic was established, approved by referendum and endowed with a constitution

3

that was intended to avert the frequent changes of government that plagued its predecessor. But, alas, the brave new republic soon proved almost as feeble as the old. It fell victim to the incessant feuding between the various parties — Socialists, Radicals, Christian Democrats and others — that made up its shifting, transient coalitions. During the 12 years the Fourth Republic survived, from 1946 to 1958, there were more than 20 different governments. One of its few forceful prime ministers was Pierre Mendès-France, a member of the Radical Party who came to power in 1954; but even he lasted in office for only seven months, having failed to secure adequate consensus for his planned reforms.

The France of the Fourth Republic was sometimes misleadingly described as "the sick man of Europe." Behind the façade of political chaos, however, the country was making steady economic progress and repairing the ravages of wartime. This rebuilding was above all due to the work of the civil service, and especially of the state agency known as the *Commissariat au Plan*, or Planning Board, which was founded in 1946 by the great administrator and statesman Jean Monnet who piloted a series of five-year plans for modernizing France. The plans provided focus and direction for the nation's machinery of government and orchestrated the efforts of the civil servants, who in a sense ruled France more than the politicians. Some of them were staid bureaucrats ensuring a smooth administration; others were dynamic, new-style technocrats, determined to haul the nation into the modern age.

In retrospect, the period of the Fourth Republic can be seen as one of profound change and growth, but at

the time observers were more aware of the chaotic spectacle of governmental instability and indecision that it presented. Its downfall was prompted by its inability to solve the country's colonial problems.

In 1954, France beat an ignominious, if inevitable, retreat from Indochina, after a crushing defeat at Dien Bien Phu at the hands of the Communist-led nationalists of the Vietminh. That same year, an insurrection broke out in Algeria, a country that was much closer to the French homeland and that numbered more than a million French settlers among its 11 million population. For the next four years, successive governments were determined that Algeria must always remain French and they poured in troops to try to defeat the Muslim liberation forces. At the same time, however, some politicians

began to recognize privately that sooner or later France would have to come to terms with Algerian aspirations. The army chiefs did not agree, nor did the settlers. In May 1958, when a new government seemed ready to negotiate with the rebels, the French forces in Algeria threatened to defy the authority of Paris and to invade France itself unless the principle of French Algeria was upheld. Civil war loomed. It was by far the worst French crisis since 1940.

At this dangerous juncture, many French people felt that only one man could save the situation and restore unity — France's wartime hero, General de Gaulle. After presiding over the provisional government that had preceded the establishment of the Fourth Republic, he had largely withdrawn from active politics and had been living at his home in the village of Colombey-

A PRESIDENTIAL SYSTEM OF GOVERNMENT

Under the Fifth Republic, France has adopted a presidential system of government that firmly separates the executive and legislative powers. The business of running the country is primarily the responsibility of the president, elected directly by popular mandate for a seven-year term. He appoints a prime minister, who in turn advises him on the choice of a council of ministers. The president is expected to set the broad outlines of national policy, which the government then administers.

The legislative branch consists of two houses: the National Assembly, elected directly for a five-year term; and the indirectly elected Senate, which can delay legislation but not initiate it. The Council of Ministers is responsible for its handling of the administration to the Assembly, which can if necessary topple the government by a vote of censure.

Local government has a three-tier structure, with three democratically elected councils. At the lowest level, municipal councils administer France's 36,000 communes. At the higher levels, separate councils represent the 96 departments and 22 regions, each of which groups two or more departments. Since the transfer of power to local governments in 1982, the local authorities at each level have enjoyed more executive and financial powers.

PRESIDENT OF THE REPUBLIC

PRIME MINISTER

COUNCIL OF MINISTERS

NATIONAL ASSEMBLY

SENATE

REGIONAL COUNCILS

DEPARTMENTAL COUNCILS

ELECTORAL COLLEGE

MUNICIPAL COUNCILS

MAYORS

ELECTORATE

◻ DIRECT ELECTION   ◻ INDIRECT ELECTION   ◻ APPOINTMENT

les-deux-Églises, in the Haute-Marne department some 120 miles east of Paris. He had played no part in the army plot against Paris, nor did he share the generals' views on French Algeria. But he did feel strongly that political parties were incapable of ruling France adequately. Instead he believed the constitution should be changed to introduce a system of rule by a president with executive powers.

De Gaulle had long believed that one

day he might be summoned back to power, so when the call eventually came, he was ready for action.

Few people had any illusions about the fact that France was being forced to change its system of government under the threat of a military coup. But at least the democratic legalities were still observed. The existing government resigned, and on June 1, 1958, the National Assembly elected de Gaulle as Prime Minister. His main condition was

the setting up of a new constitution, to establish presidential government on a seven-year mandate, and this was duly approved by referendum in September. In December, de Gaulle was elected to serve as President. Thus, with little mourning for its predecessor, the Fifth Republic was born.

During his years in power, from 1958 to 1969, de Gaulle achieved much for France. First, he managed to bring the Algerian war to an end. In the belief

3

that independence was inevitable and that the end justified the means, he in effect set about double-crossing those of his own supporters who had ingenuously taken him for a champion of French Algeria. He initiated talks with the Algerian nationalists that led to freedom for that country in 1962. Several times the army and the settlers staged revolts in bids to thwart him, but they failed. Most of the settlers were repatriated to France.

Second, de Gaulle revived the nation's self-confidence and prestige in world affairs. Besides restoring political stability, he pursued an assertive foreign policy centered on the concept of a French-led Europe, and also took measures to stabilize the franc, which had been rendered almost worthless by devaluation. Third, with the additional authority of his new office, he im-

plemented some necessary economic and social reforms that had proved too much for the weak governments of the Fourth Republic. Some of these reforms were major projects, such as schemes for modernizing agriculture and improving the school system. Others were slighter but symptomatic of the new mood in France under Gaullism — for example, a decree obliging Parisians to clean their gray and grimy housefronts, thus bringing back brightness to a city grown drab.

Not everyone warmed to de Gaulle's arrogance and authoritarianism, and many felt that he put too much stress on prestige projects and a false concept of grandeur. But most Frenchmen today would accept that his overall record was positive. He introduced a technocratic style of government rather different from that of the Fourth Republic.

Many of his senior ministers were not career politicians but men selected from outside politics, mainly from the civil service. Two of his most effective ministers, Edgar Pisani and Pierre Sudreau, were former prefects; among his prime ministers, Georges Pompidou came from a banking background, and Maurice Couve de Murville was a diplomat. De Gaulle therefore renewed France's political personnel, whose ever-recurring faces had grown all too familiar under the Fourth Republic.

In addition, he ruled very often by decree and he took scant notice of parliament (he never hid his contempt for political parties, even including his own, the Gaullists). This disdain was widely criticized as undemocratic. But de Gaulle had his own concept of democracy, which was to appeal directly to the people on important issues by means of referenda. He held five of these in all, and won the first four handsomely. Finally, though, the tactic turned against him, because in April 1969 he lost a referendum on regional and Senate reform. Taking the result personally as a vote of no confidence, he resigned. At 78 he was showing his age, and most of the nation accepted his decision without objection.

The next President was Georges Pompidou, a close lieutenant of de Gaulle's who broadly continued his policies and led France through a serene period of booming prosperity. Upon his death in 1974, the electorate, in a reformist mood, turned to a non-Gaullist, Valéry Giscard d'Estaing, an enigmatic figure who began his period of office in a blaze of liberalism but was later deflected into the priority task of tackling the economic crisis caused by the world recession of the late 1970s. At the end of his mandate in 1981, he was

Resplendent in Louis XV uniforms worn for a state ceremony, cavalry of the Republican Guard pass the Apollo Fountain in the gardens of Versailles Palace. The Guard as a prestige force maintains security in official buildings and carries out ceremonial and escort duties.

DE GAULLE: COMMUNICATOR WITH MAJESTIC STYLE

Displaying his charisma as an orator, President de Gaulle addresses an audience in Bonn during a 1962 tour of West Germany. De Gaulle's forceful use of the mass media was a primary source of his popularity, leading one commentator to describe him as "France's foremost TV star."

As France's leader between 1958 and 1969, Charles de Gaulle tried to rule as far as possible by direct mandate, preferring referenda to debates in parliament to settle controversial issues. By nature remote and aloof, he needed to develop a rapport with the people, whose political will he took it upon himself to represent.

He did so by making full use of his skill as a communicator in a succession of tours, speeches, press conferences and broadcasts.

To maximize his effectiveness, he memorized his texts, took lessons in diction and rehearsed television speeches in front of a mirror. He also exploited the government's virtual monopoly of broadcasting. In October 1962, for example, he went on television to argue his case for electing the president by direct universal suffrage, a plan opposed by the National Assembly. In a referendum, 62 per cent of voters supported him, and direct election for the presidency is still in force.

defeated in the polls by François Mitterrand, a Socialist. After 23 years of right-of-center rule, France swung to the left, and Mitterrand embarked on a major program of reforms.

De Gaulle's presidential system survived these changes and is still in force today. It is a controversial order that differs in many ways from such other familiar models as the American. The president is elected by direct universal suffrage, and is both head of state and executive head of government. He can be reelected for a second term; but if he dies or retires while still in office, there is a new election, for he has no vice president to step into his shoes. His official residence, located in the fashionable heart of Paris' Right Bank, is the Élysée Palace, formerly the home of Louis XV's mistress, Madame de Pompadour. There he is surrounded by much protocol and ceremonial trappings, among them the silver-helmeted troops of cavalrymen of the Garde Républicaine. Attempts made by Giscard to lighten the formality surrounding the palace, for example, by appearing in public in shirtsleeves and inviting garbage collectors to breakfast at the Élysée, were not much appreciated; on the whole, the French public prefer their presidents to retain a lofty dignity.

The president appoints the prime minister, who in turn advises him over the appointment of a team of cabinet ministers that can vary in number from a dozen or so to nearly 50. The division of power between president and prime minister can be equivocal and a cause of conflict. Essentially, the president lays down the main lines of policy, while his prime minister ensures they are carried out by communicating with the various ministries. Under a precedent established by de Gaulle, however, the president retains direct control over foreign affairs and defense, personally supervising the foreign minister.

Relations between the president and the prime minister vary with the personalities involved. They are normally smooth when the president picks a man who is personally loyal to him. But if the prime minister disagrees with the president's policies, or dislikes him, or has ambitions to be in the Élysée himself, then there can be intense rivalry and conflict. Such was the case between Giscard and the Gaullist Jacques Chirac, Prime Minister from 1974 to 1976. The president can always change his prime minister, and often does so.

The prime minister has two masters, for he is also answerable to parliament. This consists of two houses: a National Assembly of some 491 deputies, elected by direct vote for a five-year term; and the Senate, an upper house with 317 senators elected for a nine-year term by local councilors. The Senate can amend bills passed to it by the Assembly, but does not have the same degree of legislative power as the lower house. Relations between president and Assembly are ambiguous, because both are elected with a popular mandate; but the president has the right to dissolve the Assembly when he wishes (though not more than once every 12 months). The constitution also gives him the power, in the event of a grave national crisis, to employ special powers and rule dictatorially — a clause that was called into play only once in the first quarter century of the Fifth Republic, by de Gaulle when he was faced with an army revolt in Algeria in 1961.

The presidential system devised by de Gaulle has on the whole worked well and proved popular with the French. De Gaulle tailored the system to suit himself, a military man of potent authority, and there remains a danger that presidential control could become less effective under a weaker or less charismatic figure. Even as it is, some of the French people think that the constitution allows the president too much power by giving him direct control of the administration, thereby strengthening state centralism. It is also sometimes argued that when the president and the majority of the National Assembly are of the same political color, as is usually the case, parliament tends to become a mere rubber stamp, approving all the president's designs. Certainly the French parliament has less influence on the governing of the country than, say, its British equivalent or Congress in the United States.

And yet, if president and Assembly were of opposite colors, there could be serious conflict. The mandates of the two seldom coincide, since the president is elected for seven years and the Assembly for five. This might one day lead to the president having to rule in conjunction with a hostile Assembly — a situation that could, it is feared, make France virtually ungovernable, for the political divisions between left and right are sharp.

Under the Fifth Republic, the major political parties in France have fallen into four main groupings, forming two pairs linked in uneasy alliances. On the left are Socialists and Communists; on the right, Gaullists and non-Gaullists, the latter known loosely since the mid-1970s as "Giscardiens," after the president around whom they used to rally. The links between the Gaullists and "Giscardiens" are fluctuating and complex, and it is not really possible to state that either grouping stands to the right of the other. The two actually run par-

A SEASON OF REBELLION

May 1968 has gone down in history as the month when General de Gaulle's government was almost toppled by radical protest. The troubles began in the universities, where unrest had been simmering over the inadequacies of the educational system. Violence flared on May 2 at Nanterre in northwestern Paris, where the school closed following clashes during a demonstration against American intervention in Vietnam.

Protest at once spread to central Paris, where students occupied the Sorbonne the next day. To restore order, the head of the university, acting on government instructions, called in riot police. Their strong-arm tactics only escalated the conflict, which reached a peak on May 10, the so-called "Night of the Barricades," when students and police fought a pitched battle in the Latin Quarter that left 400 people injured and 200 vehicles damaged or burned out.

The revolt spread to universities across France, and soon industrial workers, nursing their own grievances over pay and working conditions, began to join the students' cause. A general strike was called for May 13. Agitation continued, and by May 25 nearly 10 million workers were idle.

It seemed that de Gaulle would be forced to resign but, on May 30, he dissolved the National Assembly and called a general election for late June. By then, a conservative backlash against the disorders had gathered force, and de Gaulle's party returned to power with an increased majority.

During one of many demonstrations in May 1968, Parisian students, masks splashed with red paint simulating blood, turn a dummy policeman upside down to protest the brutality displayed by riot police during earlier clashes.

At the height of the troubles, Parisian students set up a blazing barricade of cars during a nocturnal battle with riot police.

Supporters of General de Gaulle mass at the Arc de Triomphe on May 30.

Steel-helmeted police drive back demonstrators with tear-gas grenades.

3

allel, each attracting a wide range of supporters from reactionary right-wingers to reformist liberals. Their main differences are of historical and personal loyalties.

The Gaullist Party has changed its official name several times over the years and is now known as the R.P.R. (Rassemblement pour la République). It had as its *raison d'être* a firm support for de Gaulle and his policies until the general retired from politics in 1969; it subsequently shifted its focus to a vaguer kind of neo-Gaullism centered on the personality of its new leader, the assertive Jacques Chirac, the Mayor of Paris. The Gaullist Party is nationalist, suspicious of NATO, of European integration and of American influence. In domestic affairs, many of its leaders are socially progressive, as de Gaulle himself was. The party appeals to a wide range of voters of all classes, including many workers. Many of the party's older supporters are still motivated by a nostalgia for de Gaulle and for his ideals; younger ones are more likely to be inspired by Jacques Chirac's crusade to rescue France from the "catastrophe" of left-wing rule.

The non-Gaullists are a loose collection of groups and parties united as much as anything by a dislike of Gaullism. Some groups have their roots in the true right, based on wartime support for the collaborationist government of Marshal Pétain, while others have evolved from radically different beginnings in the liberal postwar Christian Democrat movement. In the mid-1970s, these diverse elements formed a single coalition in the center of the political spectrum, held together by the desire to support Giscard's reformism. The Giscardiens are less nationalistic than the Gaullists, but socially their vot-

ers are quite as varied, from wealthy businessmen to junior clerks and peasants. Gaullists and Giscardiens are constantly bickering; but whether in or out of power, they are always allied against their common enemy, the left.

Here, the ideological rift between Socialists and Communists runs far deeper and rivalries are much fiercer, dating back to the French Communist Party's foundation in 1920. The two parties need each other's electoral support and so are forced into partnership, yet they remain very different. The Socialist Party is open and easygoing, an amiable cacophony of voices conducting arguments in public about its policies. It is a diverse party, in which a Marxist wing can coexist with a strong social-democratic faction that wants to retain a mixed economy, combining public and private ownership. The party's fortunes have fluctuated wildly; its share of the total vote in national elections sank to 16 per cent in 1968, but by the 1981 election it had become the most popular party in France, with 36 per cent of the poll. The hard core of its electorate are workers, junior employees and teachers, but it also attracts many people from other professions and even from business milieus.

France's Communist Party, though now in decline, is still the largest in Western Europe after Italy's. In recent years it has given up the aim of taking power by way of revolution, and is also less subservient to the Soviet Union than it was in the postwar years. It remains a highly disciplined, secretive body, however, and despite brief bouts of liberalization has not really shaken off its allegiance to Soviet-style Communism. It is run from a large, modern headquarters in a working-class district of eastern Paris, known as "the bunker"

because of the austerity of its vast, concrete underground foyer. Here, decisions are taken by an oligarchy on whom the rank and file of the party have little influence.

In view of the siege mentality of its leaders, it is perhaps not surprising that the party's electoral support has been dropping slowly but steadily, from a postwar peak of 25 per cent to a low of 16 per cent in 1981. Yet many reasonable people from all the social classes go on voting for the party. Workers are attracted to it by its links with France's biggest trade union, the Confédération Générale du Travail (C.G.T.), which has always been effective in battling for better pay and conditions for its members. Older voters remember that the Communists distinguished themselves for many years in the wartime resistance to German occupation. More recently, the party has achieved a good record of local administration in the many towns where it is in power. In addition, it has always been a magnet for protest votes, and has further benefited from the old romantic French revolutionary tradition, which still causes students, intellectuals and others to make it a point of honor of voting for the far left, however set the party may have become in its ways.

Such conservatism is in itself symptomatic, because the violent, antiparliamentary extremes that used to mark French politics have waned in recent years. The fascist movements, active before and during World War II and also in the final stages of the Algerian drama, have faded from political life. The militant left-wing groups, too, who were so vocal in the student uprising of May 1968, have since departed from the limelight. But if these challenges to democracy have been reduced, another fundamental problem remains: the division of the nation into two hostile blocs of right and left, making consensus on almost any issue difficult to achieve. Because of the rift, the center fails to make much of an impact in politics, even though that is where a high proportion of ordinary French people really belong.

This polarization has made the alternation of power that is normal in a healthy democracy harder. Indeed, one reason right-of-center governments stayed in power continuously for 23 years in France, from de Gaulle's return to power in 1958 until the Socialist victory of 1981, was the fear on the part of the electorate that, because of the gulf between left and right, change would be hazardous. When it finally came, however, the transfer of power passed smoothly. In the civil service, the Socialists changed a number of personnel in key positions, as was expected, but the state institutions continued to function normally. Most civil servants calmly set about working for their new, leftist masters, and political change was accommodated without any major upheaval.

Continuity in the administration is vital to the well-being of France since the government depends upon the upper echelons of the civil service to supervise the running of the nation, as in many other countries. But the way in which the top level of bureaucrats is recruited is uniquely French, relying on a complex, meritocratic system by which many of the levers of power remain in the hands of a dozen or so state agencies known as *les grands corps de l'état* (major state corps). Each corps has a specific role — for example, to audit state accounts — but more importantly

they serve as pools of talent to supply both state and industry with top-level administrators. These small and self-perpetuating bodies dominate much of public life in a land where the technocrat has, at least since the Revolution of 1789, been a powerful figure.

The corps have their roots in the French educational system. The upper ranks of the civil service and of the main state technical agencies are largely recruited not from the universities, which have relatively low prestige, but from a handful of smaller and more exclusive state colleges known as the *grandes écoles* (major schools). Of these, the most influential are the École Polytechnique, an engineering school now situated in the Paris suburbs, which was founded by Napoleon and is still run on

semi-military lines; and the new École Nationale d'Administration (whose acronym is ENA), a graduate college in central Paris which was created in 1945 to train future senior civil servants. The top 10 to 15 per cent of alumni of these two schools then join the *grands corps.* Once co-opted into one of these privileged fraternities, they can expect to remain members for life, although they continue to retain the right to work elsewhere should they so desire. Membership in the *grands corps* is similar to belonging to an exclusive club.

The corps fall into two rival camps, the "technical" and the "administrative." The former include the prestigious Corps des Ponts et Chaussées, dealing with bridges, roads and other public works; they are led by engineers from the École Polytechnique. Many of these technocrats — most of them are men, though now a few women are included — may eventually move from the corps to take top jobs in state agencies such as the S.N.C.F., which runs the railway network; or they may go into key jobs in nationalized industries, such as the Renault car manufacturers or even into private firms. These *polytechniciens* — nicknamed *les X* because of the crossed-cannon badge of their school — form a powerful clan with strong old-boy loyalties; a *polytechnicien* will usually try to fill a top vacancy on his staff with a fellow "X."

The "administrative" corps, mainly recruited from ENA, are even more influential, for they have a greater impact on politics. The most important of these corps are the Conseil d'État, which advises on legal disputes, the Inspection des Finances and the Cour des Comptes, both of which verify public accounts. But the ambitious young entrant will probably not spend long at

3

such routine work; more likely he will use the prestige of the corps, and the freedom and scope it offers, as the springboard for a public career. Perhaps he will join some minister's personal staff and enter politics himself; or he may climb swiftly up the ladder of civil service promotion. Many of the leading French politicians have corps connections — for example, Jacques Chirac, the Gaullist leader, who entered the Cour des Comptes, or Giscard himself, a supreme product of the system: He graduated both from the École Polytechnique and then from ENA, going on to join the 300-member Inspection des Finances.

Outlining the career of a typical *inspecteur* may serve to illustrate the freedom in changing jobs that makes the system so attractive to its beneficiaries. Pierre Achard was born in Paris in 1934, the son of a writer. He attended one of the better Parisian state secondary schools before entering ENA. There he did well enough in the competitive final examinations to opt for a place in the Inspection. "I chose this career," he said, "because I have a sense of service to my country. Also, I admit, the pay is pretty good." After spending an obligatory initial term of four years within the ranks of the Inspection itself, where he was principally occupied in checking on the way public money was spent in the city of Orléans, he was able to branch out into other administrative fields. First he took a government post dealing with European Economic Community (EEC) affairs — he is a devoted supporter of the Common Market — then he served on the personal staffs of two ministers.

He could have used the experience gained to pursue a political career of his own, but he rejected the opportunity.

Instead, he entered the diplomatic field as a financial counselor in Bonn, West Germany, before moving back to a more senior EEC post. When the Left came to power in 1981, he felt politically ill at ease in a government job, so he decided to return to the routine work of the Inspection, as he had an automatic right to do. An *inspecteur des finances* is never to be found on the dole.

The system, so convenient for its proteges, also has numerous advantages for the nation as a whole. The corps attracts many of the nation's finest brains, providing an elite civil service of high quality whose members are well paid and usually have a lofty sense of public duty. The flexibility of the system provides a valuable reserve of top-level talent, enabling a clever, energetic newcomer to make diverse use of his abilities in its service — and often at a young age, when he is full of ideas and a zest for reform. Moreover, since corps members are spread across a wide range of jobs in both state-run and private enterprises, from government ministries to banks and private firms, the mesh of close personal links created is invaluable in short-circuiting the bureaucratic delays that would otherwise occur. Sharing the same ethos and speaking the same language, they can work in concert to get things done.

Yet the system also has drawbacks that have exposed it to much criticism. It creates in almost every public body a gulf between the privileged upper ranks and the rest of the employees. Promotion on merit from the middle ranks is difficult to come by; students who failed to acquire the right *grande école* diploma in their youth have little chance of moving far up the hierarchy, however able they may prove themselves. This lack of prospects inevitably

leads to frustration, apathy and a lack of initiative in civil servants below the top level. Further criticisms are aimed at the selection processes for the *grandes écoles* themselves. Access is in theory open to all, and the examinations that determine entry to, and graduation from, the schools are fair and impartial. In practice, however, those accepted are predominantly from the middle class, and — in the case of ENA — Parisian. Children from cultured family backgrounds are inevitably better equipped than others for the ultracompetitive entry examination.

Another frequent complaint is that the average *énarque*, as ENA graduates are called, has little contact with the realities of daily life, however bright and vigorous he may be, for he goes straight into an administrative desk job on leaving college. Having little contact with the people, the technocrat is often seen as aloof and impersonal, arrogantly imposing his decisions in the sure belief that he knows best. Recent attempts have been made to reform the system in order to meet some of these criticisms — notably by broadening the schools' intake — but it remains to be seen whether they are going to have any marked effect on the administration of the nation.

The local government system through which the politicians and civil servants govern France is also, and more profoundly, in a state of flux. It has a three-tier structure. At the bottom level, the nation is divided into some 36,000 communes, most of them villages but including such big cities as Lyon and Bordeaux. Each of the communes has a municipal council, elected by popular vote, and a mayor chosen by the councilors from their ranks. The mayor is

Pupils of the École Polytechnique, an elite college for students of science and technology, parade in full dress on July 14, France's national holiday. Founded in 1794 to train military engineers, the school still has a soldierly flavor, but most graduates enter industry or public service.

usually a person of some local influence, and he is the official representative of the state in his area. Since 1982, mayors have received salaries for their work, giving them more time to concentrate on the job.

The middle tier of administration consists of the 96 departments, most of them named after geographical features such as rivers—Seine-et Marne and Tarn-et-Garonne, for example. Above them are the 22 regions, into which France has been administratively divided since 1964, each of them containing several departments. Departments have for a long time been administered by directly elected councils. When the Socialists came to power in 1981, the centerpiece of their decentralization reform program was to introduce direct elections for the 22 regions as well.

These reforms, described at the time by then-Prime Minister Pierre Mauroy as "the main business" of the Mitterrand presidency, aimed at a major transfer of power from Paris to the rest of the country. An important part of the program was a diminution of the authority of the prefects. Guardians of the interests of the state, these officials had hitherto strictly curtailed the freedom of action of the local councils by their careful tutelage. The prefects' tasks included keeping law and order, controlling most of the local police

3

Under a bust of Marianne, a symbol of the Republic, members of a municipal council in a village in Normandy settle down to business. The councils, financed by government subsidy and by local taxes, elect their own mayors — local dignitaries who often retain power for decades.

force, supervising the communes within their jurisdiction and coordinating the activities of the various government ministries and their agencies within their borders. The prefects traditionally lived in grand style in majestic prefectures established in each departmental capital. There they would put on lavish entertainments, presiding over dinners and receptions in ornate blue-and-gold uniforms. To prevent them from developing regional power bases, they were moved from post to post every few years.

The prefectural system, though often criticized for its autocracy, had many strengths in its favor; it provided stability in times of unrest and also helped the state to initiate bold economic projects in the regions. Yet over the years it had come to symbolize Parisian interference in local affairs, and its authority was increasingly resented. Under the Socialist reforms, the prefects' title was changed to "Commissioners of the Republic," and although they were allowed their uniforms and some ceremonial duties, their real powers were much reduced.

Under the new order, communes no longer have to submit their budgets to the prefects for scrutiny; instead, the state's contribution to local government financing is now to go directly to the mayor and his council as a lump sum. At the same time the powers of the regions and of the departments have been increased. The planned division of responsibility between the various tiers of local government is for the regions to look after economic planning and cultural affairs; the departments are to look after various welfare and administrative matters, and the communes will take charge of their own housing, environment and services.

However, the state is to retain control of the larger national projects such as nuclear energy.

The transfer of power from Paris represented by the reforms is only one aspect of a more general revival in the provinces, which have been reasserting themselves to a remarkable extent demographically, economically and culturally as well as politically. The immediate postwar days when experts used the phrase "the French desert" to describe the wasteland beyond Paris are long since gone. The process began even during the war years, when the hold of Paris was weakened by the division of the nation into two zones, occupied and not occupied, and the transfer of power over the latter to a new capital in central France, Vichy. Then after 1945 several new factors came together

to favor the growing importance of the provinces — the mass rural exodus to the cities, the upsurge in the birth rate and the industrial boom.

For once Paris was not able to hog all the new wealth and activity; the suburban spread still grew, but far slower than in other cities, many of which doubled or tripled their populations in the decades after the war. The government itself helped the revival, by a concerted policy of encouraging new industries to settle in the provinces and by enticing existing ones to move out of Paris. Several of the *grandes écoles* were transferred from the capital. Even the transportation network became less focused on Paris; at last it ceased to be faster for a resident of Toulouse to go by train to Lyon by taking a detour to Paris — a distance of 648 miles — than to go on the direct, 330-mile cross-country route.

Cities such as Rennes and Grenoble, previously sleepy and sluggish, have become vibrant with new life in the form of modern factories and fast-growing universities. Nor has culture been left behind. Paris has begun to lose her artistic and intellectual near-monopoly; indeed, France's postwar theater and music renaissance has been especially striking in the provinces. At the same time, the old antiprovincial snobbery of the Parisian bourgeoisie has begun to be replaced by an anti-Parisian snobbery, at least among the young people. Modern pressures have made life so frenetic in the capital that some executives will happily migrate to a smaller city, especially if it is situated in the sunny south. By a strange reversal of attitudes, it is now almost more chic to live and work in, say, Avignon than in Paris' Montparnasse.

Another aspect of the revival has been an upsurge in regional self-awareness, especially in provinces such as Brittany, Languedoc or Alsace with a strong historical and ethnic identity. It is a trend shared with other parts of Europe — from Scotland to Catalonia — in an age when people are turning back to local loyalties and traditions in reaction against the uniformity of modern consumer society. In France, the revival has meant a new interest in folklore, traditional customs and regional dialects. Often the movement is led by the young.

The provincial revival and the reforms in local government together can be seen as reactions against the old tradition of centralized power, which has been increasingly called into question in the decades of peace and prosperity since World War II. Yet for the trend to gather momentum, a fundamental

change would have to occur in French life. There is still a tendency to expect the state to take the initiative for almost any social venture, however limited in scope, even down to the level of starting a local community center; if it fails to do so, the backers of the project are more likely to sign angry petitions of protest rather than try and raise the money needed themselves. Yet some such habit of direct citizen participation in administration will be necessary if the old system is ever to be substantially altered. Happily, there have been signs of just such a development in the new emphasis laid on what the French call *la vie associative:* spontaneous local cooperation to seek remedies to specific problems. Such a movement can only come from the grass roots; it remains to be seen if it will grow. □

On a wall with the slogan "Colonists out," a supporter of the now-banned Corsican National Liberation Front waves a flag bearing a Moor's head, Corsica's heraldic device since 1761 and the separatist movement's symbol. Various groups of separatists lead a vocal, often violent minority.

THE LEGACY OF THE BOOM YEARS

A convoy of tractors ferries artichokes to a cooperative in Brittany. The formation of such cooperatives, which cut out middlemen and increased profits for growers, was one of the sweeping postwar changes that transformed the country's agriculture into a modern and efficient industry.

René Hémon left school at 13. As a farmer's son in the 1930s he had started work even before that age, for on his father's small property on the edge of the wealthy Beauce wheat plains, southwest of Paris, there was always work to be done after classes were over: root vegetables to cut for the cows, hay to collect for the horses, pigsties to be cleaned. As René wryly puts it now, "Working was how I relaxed."

In those days the Hémon family never imagined that their life could be otherwise. But time has proved them wrong. Since he took over the farm at the end of the war, René has seen the business of agriculture — for it has become such — and the whole economy of France change faster than at any other period in its history. Indeed, few economies anywhere have undergone such deep and rapid transformation.

René's own family is an example. When he retires, there will be no more Hémons on the farm. The parents saved to send their four sons to a private boarding school in La Vendée. The eldest, François, went straight from the school to an engineering college in Paris, and then took a job in the capital. Now he is an engineer in a subsidiary of the car manufacturing firm Renault, working in the new town of Evry on the outskirts of Paris. Jean-Louis, a year younger, is a teacher of mentally handicapped children in Nantes. The third son, Jacques, is a journalist. Only the youngest in the family, Marc, still retains any interest in agriculture. He is studying biology in La Rochelle; when he graduates, he hopes to specialize in soil analysis.

The Hémons take pride in the fact that all their children have been able to develop their aptitudes to the fullest. Yet René views their new lives away from the farm a little wistfully. "Youngsters working in town are very single-minded," he says. "They want a job, a car, a second home, a vacation — not all the uncertainties about tomorrow that go with farming." Like most Frenchmen, he naturally accepts the fact that his children have come to expect a way of living that their ancestors would hardly have dreamed of.

That is perhaps the most striking element in the story of a family which, from father to sons, spans France's progression from an agricultural to an industrial society, and now to the start of a postindustrial one. The preconditions for such a transformation have existed for a long time. France has always had its share of inventors and innovators. Joseph-Nicéphore Niepce and Jacques Daguerre invented photography in the first half of the 19th Century. Alexandre-Gustave Eiffel's tower, built in 1889, is not just the symbol of Paris but, for the time of its construction, a miracle of engineering. Louis Blériot and Roland Garros were pioneers of aviation. Nor has the country ever been deficient in natural resources: Farmland and forests abound

4

Cars queue nose to tail on the *périphérique*, the beltway built in the 1970s to keep through traffic out of central Paris. Despite over 3,000 miles of highway built between 1967 and 1980, car ownership doubled in the same period, resulting in sporadic traffic congestion.

throughout France, coal is found in the north and east and around the fringes of the Massif Central, iron ore underlies the eastern province of Lorraine. In addition, its administrations have been promoting industrial development for centuries. Some of the oldest and most renowned producers, including the Sèvres porcelain and Gobelin tapestry factories, owe their existence to royal patronage, and are now state-owned.

Yet despite its rich human and physical potential, France lagged behind the United States, Britain and Germany in terms of economic progress until World War II. Names such as Sèvres and Gobelin — or Aubusson, famed for its carpets, or Chantilly and its lace — offer a clue to what went wrong. The nation has a long tradition of high craftsmanship for luxury goods, but until recently lagged behind in large-scale production for everyday needs. In America, Britain and Germany, the industrial revolution fed and was fed by the explosive growth of mass markets in the newly prosperous towns and cities. France did not have that growth. In the 150 years leading up to 1945, its population grew by only 13 million people — no more than in the 30 years from 1945 to 1975.

One fact and one set of figures go a long way to explain why the French economy remained relatively stagnant. France's rich farmland was not just a resource, but a trap, and in the 1890s the French closed it upon themselves. The government decided to keep out food imports, which were undercutting the prices of native farm produce. Secure against competition, the farmers then went on peaceably in their old, inefficient ways while the world changed around them. The rich land continued to provide a poor living for millions of peasants — millions who could have been more gainfully employed in industry. In 1906, there were nearly nine million agricultural workers, almost 45 per cent of the working population. Forty years later, at the end of World War II, there were still 7.5 million, 36 per cent of all those at work.

Then came radical change. By the early 1960s, the number of people working the land had halved. By the mid-1970s, the figure had halved again. Today less than 8 per cent of the working population are employed on the farms. Millions were released for other work, constituting a vast untapped labor force that was swelled still further as the postwar baby boom brought new consumers and, later, new workers into the market.

And work was easy to find. France, like Germany, had seen its industry and transport devastated in World War II. A huge task of reconstruction and modernization awaited. Housing in particular demanded immediate attention, for France had built pitifully few houses between the wars.

The nation set about reconstruction with a will. The necessary capital was provided in part by American money that flowed in after 1947 as Marshall aid — so called after General George Marshall, who had devised the plan to refloat Europe's war-devastated economies with massive cash infusions. France's share amounted to some $2.8 billion. To coordinate redevelopment, an organization called the National Planning Board was established, under the leadership of a man of unusual vision and determination, Jean Monnet. The blueprint that he devised — the first of a succession of five-year plans

that have guided the French economy
up to the present day — gave priority to
the reconstruction of heavy industry.

The result was a remarkable success.
From the late 1940s until 1973, when
the decision by member states of the
Organization of Petroleum-Exporting
Countries (OPEC) to double the price
of oil buffeted Western economies with
the first shock of the oil crisis, France
enjoyed 25 almost uninterrupted boom
years. National output grew three and a
half times, at an average rate of more
than 5 per cent a year. Growth was far
faster than at any previous period in
French history, and outpaced most of
the competing countries, even at a time
when the whole world was on an economic upswing.

The statistics for such key industries
as automobiles and construction were
even more impressive. At the start of

the 1960s, France was manufacturing
about 1.2 million cars a year. By the early 1970s, the figure was almost three
million, around half of those for the export market. After that the number
rose slowly, then dropped. But France
continued to rival West Germany in
automobile production, while Britain,
in contrast, lagged far behind.

Between the wars, France never built
more than 200,000 houses annually,
and usually around half that number.
Rent controls imposed at the start of
World War I discouraged development. In 1948, the figure for housing
starts was as low as 62,000. But then the
government freed rents on new properties, and the number soared immediately: Over 300,000 houses were started in 1960, more than 400,000 in 1970,
a peak of 550,000 in 1974, and still
some 400,000 in the first half of the

1980s, recession notwithstanding.

The government then turned its attention to constructing *autoroutes* and
later to modernizing the telephone system. As late as 1960, France had less
than 120 miles of modern highways; by
1980 the total distance had risen to over
3,000 miles. The telephone system
used to be the despair of French business and a favorite subject for humor-
ists: There was a familiar joke that half
of France was waiting for a telephone
and the other half for a dial tone. As
late as 1970, France had only 4.25 million lines — eight for every 100 inhabitants and about a third of the figure for
comparable countries. But then President Pompidou decided that the joke
had gone on long enough. At enormous cost, the number of lines was increased to 6.5 million by 1975 and 16
million by 1981, with eight million
more planned for the mid-1980s. The
nation now has one of Europe's most
modern systems.

More surprisingly, output increased in
René Hémon's profession, farming,
despite the drift of workers from the
land. Figures tell part of the story. Before 1939, France produced between
10 and 12 million tons of grain each
year. By the start of the 1970s, the harvest topped 36 million tons, nearly 25
per cent of it corn, a crop almost unknown 20 years before, and the ton-
nage continued to grow throughout the
decade. Fertilizer use multiplied by
three in two decades. As late as 1950,
France had more than two million
farms but only 150,000 tractors. By
1973, there were only 1.3 million
farms — and 1.3 million tractors.

The revolution in the ways of country life was inspired by the farm prices
guaranteed by the EEC and by the bold

A combine harvester cuts a swath through a wheatfield in the Ile de France, one of the country's main producers of grain. The grainfields of the north have been pacesetters of agricultural modernization, with the average size of farms doubling between 1955 and 1980.

leadership of the farmers themselves. An important improvement on traditional practices was *remembrement,* the regrouping of fields. In the past, French inheritance laws had required land to be divided among a farmer's children upon his death, with the result that many farms had become scattered collections of fields, often miles away from each other. After 1945, in many areas, these diffuse holdings were brought together again by a series of complicated exchanges, which were subsidized by the government. By these, a farmer would lose some land in one place, but be recompensed with extra land adjoining the main part of his property, thereby saving time and energy in efficiently exploiting his property. The Hémons initiated just such a scheme in their district in 1959, and used it to consolidate their holdings.

In addition to *remembrement,* organizations were set up with first option to buy farmland coming onto the market, sometimes at preemptive prices, which was then resold on favorable credit terms to help young farmers acquire land, and also to enlarge existing farms. Special grants made it possible for elderly farmers to retire, and the Crédit Agricole, the farmers' bank, adopted an easy-loan policy so that farmers could borrow the money that was needed to modernize their implements and farming methods.

Meanwhile, the farmers themselves were not idle. A remarkable new breed of reformers had come to the fore in the immediate postwar years. Inspired by the radical Catholicism of the Jeunesse Agricole Chrétienne, the Christian Agricultural Youth, a body founded in 1929 to promote Christianity in the countryside, they took over strategic positions in the traditionally conservative farmers' unions, converting them into mouthpieces for their own views. Their goal was nothing less than the structural reorganization of French farming. One of their principal targets was the antiquated marketing system that saw much of the profits generated by French agriculture falling into the hands of wholesalers rather than the farmers themselves. On this issue they were prepared to accept rioting as a way of bringing about change. They lent their support to the vegetable growers of Brittany when they turned to violence in order to protect low prices in 1961. At Pont l'Abbé, farmers protesting the collapse of potato prices poured tons of their crop, sprayed with gasoline to make it inedible, across a main street, while at Morlaix 4,000 vegetable growers took control of a sub-prefecture to draw the government's attention to their grievances.

Besides exerting pressure on the government, the reformers also took initiatives of their own, notably by setting up marketing cooperatives all over France to cut out middlemen in selling their produce. Most of these ventures were successful. In Normandy, for instance, the big dairy cooperatives grew to be as large and well managed as many an industrial company. One of them now controls one eighth of national milk production and runs more than 40 factories; another produces and distributes one of the nation's best-known brands of yogurt.

Their efforts and those of the government combined to alter the face of French agriculture. The numbers of farmers declined as individuals with small properties, many of them part-timers, sold out or retired without heirs to take over their holdings. Farm sizes grew. By 1980, around half a million of

France's 1.2 million holdings were more than 50 acres in extent, with more than 150,000 of these above 125 acres. Well over four fifths of France's agricultural land had become grouped in these large properties.

René Hémon's personal experience exemplifies the trend. His father had started with 45 acres in 1939 — already a sizable estate for France as a whole, though not for the Beauce, an area of large landholdings — and slowly built the figure up to 113 acres. René, in joint ownership with his brother-in-law, now has 375 acres, 250 of these former woodland that he bought and cleared himself.

The Hémons' property is now large even for the Beauce. In other areas of France, particularly in the south, such an estate is still rare. There the problems are different, and progress has been slower. In Languedoc and Provence, the growers of peaches and tomatoes and, above all, the makers of wine — mostly producer cooperatives, not the great vineyards, which account for only a tiny part of France's output — have had to cope with the threat of overproduction and of cheap imports from Italy. The farm riots in the early 1960s were led by Bretons; from the mid-1970s on it has generally been the far south that riots.

The changes in farm life since the war have had sad results in the central uplands too, where many small villages are almost deserted. Only special state aid keeps the sheepfarmers who inhabit them in business, and those who survive live hardly better than their fathers did before them. Although the system of price fixing by the EEC has brought many benefits to French farming as a whole, the greater part has been reaped by the large-scale farmers in the north;

smaller producers elsewhere, in districts where extensive grain production is impossible, have gained relatively little from it.

The gap between rich and poor farmers has tended to widen further as the amount of capital needed to buy new machinery and stay competitive in an increasingly cutthroat market grows. René Hémon has seen the overhead expenses incurred in running the family farm spiral alarmingly upward. His father could just about earn a living on 45 acres, he says; now he reckons that 200 acres is the minimum necessary, and he forecasts that soon 375 acres will be needed for one man to make a decent living.

For the time being, however, he has little to complain of in the quality of his own daily life and in that of his sons. He and his wife have an attractive old house with a large garden full of fruit trees, and they can afford to take vacations outside France, in Switzerland, Germany and Yugoslavia. In place of the horse-drawn baler that his father used to bring in the crops, he has a combine harvester, and he drives an ultra-modern tractor with a radio and air conditioning in the cab. Their children live equally well, for the true distinction in living standards today is no longer, as it once was, between town and country, but between the past and the present; so much so that the life lived by previous generations of their own family on the farm would now seem to them frighteningly deprived.

To explain the unparalleled levels of growth that underlay the rise in French living standards, economists have concentrated on two very different factors — the role of economic planning and the expansion of markets for

4

French goods. Until the oil crisis shook the nation, conventional wisdom gave much of the credit to adept governmental handling of the economy, for state intervention was pervasive in the years after the war.

Its most obvious manifestation was a wave of nationalizations launched in 1945. The Liberation brought Socialists, and for a time Communists, into the government, and they were happy to increase the public sector of the economy, often at the expense of managements tainted by the charge of collaborating with the occupying German army. General de Gaulle, as head of the government, approved. A soldier by training, he believed far more in the authority of the state than in the freedom of the market; and the belief that the authorities in Paris should take the lead in economic direction was no modern innovation in France, but a tradition firmly established even before the Revolution of 1789, in the days of the *ancien régime*. As a result, coal, gas, electricity and the Renault car company were nationalized. So were the major insurance companies, the Bank of France and three big private commercial banks, enabling the state to push capital for investment where it chose.

In general, the nationalized enterprises continued to perform well. As a result, the right-wing presidents of the Fifth Republic — de Gaulle and his successors, Georges Pompidou and Valéry Giscard d'Estaing — denationalized nothing. Pompidou, indeed, was more receptive than de Gaulle to the open-market policies; even though he brought in private capital to modernize France's telephones and highways, he never considered releasing the state hold on them or on other parts of its industrial empire. Giscard sometimes talked like a doctrinaire believer in free enterprise, and under his presidency Prime Minister Raymond Barre, a former economics professor, set about removing the price controls that remained from the protectionist prewar era. When he set free the amount that bakers could charge for the *baguette,* France's familiar, long, thin loaf of bread, it was indeed the first time that its cost had not been artificially held down with the aid of government subsidies for more than a century. Yet it was also in Giscard's term of office that the state effectively took control of two giant steel companies, admittedly not from choice but to save them from financial collapse. So when the Socialist François Mitterrand carried out another wave of nationalizations in the early 1980s, criticism from the right-wing opponents made little impression.

Nor did the state confine its economic activity to the various companies it owned. From the earliest postwar days, it tried to steer investment by private companies also. It set targets and priorities for key industrial sectors, promising state backing for firms that followed its guidance in launching export drives, say, or in acquiring new technology. It picked favored firms as the main or only suppliers to state industries such as the telephone service. Governmental agencies were set up to manipulate an armory of grants and loans to encourage industry to build factories in backward regions or to tempt foreign investors to locate their European headquarters in France. State planning and state cash brought the country, among other developments, a big Ford factory near Bordeaux, giant vacation resorts on the neglected southern coast

Surplus peaches are plowed back into the land in the Rhône Valley. Such destruction is partly the result of European Economic Community agricultural policy, which guarantees high prices for farm produce and thus encourages overproduction. Surplus is destroyed or sold at low prices outside the EEC.

A grape-picking machine gathers in the crop in the Cognac region. Introduced in the 1970s, the machines harvest in a day what 12 laborers would pick in a week. They are used increasingly in nonvintage areas, but not in the great vineyards, for fear of damaging the grapes.

between the Spanish frontier and the Riviera, and a vast new steel plant at Fos, near Marseille.

It was also the state that took the lead in improving conditions for its workers. Trade unions, which in most Western democracies have provided the impetus for such reforms, have had relatively little influence in France, partly as a result of their own divisions. There are not one but three confederations competing for the average worker's loyalty — the Communist-led Confédération Générale du Travail (CGT), the pro-Socialist Confédération Français et Démocratique du Travail (CFDT), and the Social-Democratic Force Ouvrière — in addition to more specialized bodies like the left-wing FEN for teachers and the CGC for the cadres, the managerial class from foremen upward. For all this choice, only 25 per cent of French employees were unionized in 1980; the typical Western European figure at that time was about 40 per cent. Strikes in France have been mainly one- or two-day affairs at the most — pinpricks in the hide of the nation's employers.

Consequently the government was acting largely on its own initiative when it laid down an official work week of 40 hours in 1936 and a minimum wage in 1949. It also decreed a minimum vacation: In 1981, the Mitterrand administration persuaded the employers' organization, the Conseil National du Patronat Français, to agree with the unions on a basic five weeks' annual paid vacation — a period beyond the dreams of the United States, Japan or much of Europe.

The state also encouraged, oversaw and increasingly came to pay for a system of welfare benefits more generous — and more costly, as employers complain — than most in Europe. It required employers to prove need before reducing staffs. When job losses became a problem, during the presidency of Valéry Giscard d'Estaing, the government promised to make laid-off workers' unemployment benefit up to 90 per cent of their previous salary for a year — a percentage that was soon reduced as unemployment rose.

The result of so much successful governmental intervention was a pervasive belief in planning as a panacea for all economic ills. Despite the fact that its role was advisory rather than compulsory, the Plan — as the body that devised the successive five-year strategies came to be known — even developed something of a mystique when its ambitious projections continued, year after year, more or less to come true.

Then came the oil crisis, and the entire situation changed. Suddenly, business stagnated. Though it picked up again in the late 1970s, the economy only grew at about half the rate France had become accustomed to, and it collapsed again after a second round of major oil price rises in 1979 and 1980. Unemployment rose relentlessly, from well under half a million in 1970 to one million by 1975, one and a half million by 1980 and reaching two million by 1982, when attempts to reverse the trend through lavish spending by the government proved only partly successful and vastly expensive.

The recession hit traditional heavy industries particularly hard. One of the worst sufferers was steel. The steel companies loyally continued to use native raw materials throughout the 1970s, even though supplies of iron and coal could be purchased more

4

cheaply overseas. But this policy put the French producers at a cost disadvantage at a time when markets were in any case shrinking as the recession reduced demand for their product. The results in Lorraine, the industry's principal home in France, were catastrophic. Jobs were lost by the thousands, and the powerful trade-union resistance to cuts created a crisis that stirred uncomfortable memories of the troubles of May 1968. For some weeks early in 1979, the steel town of Longwy was all but controlled by striking workers.

Other industries suffered as much, if less dramatically. Shipbuilding output fell by two thirds between the mid-1970s and 1980. The famous Citroën car firm was only saved from financial ruin when it was taken over by its rival, Peugeot, and then Peugeot in its turn ran into heavy losses. The textile industry, France's second largest industrial employer as recently as the early 1970s, had to slim down, and consequently the share of the market taken by imported goods mushroomed in just eight years prior to 1981 from one third to a half.

The years of recession had a profound effect on the self-confidence of the nation. After 25 years of expansionism, economic progress slowed, and the loss of forward momentum inevitably led people to view the successes of the earlier years in a different light. The formulas that proved adequate in the past ceased to work in the new climate. Instead of receiving praise for the economy's advances, the government became a scapegoat to blame for its failings, although the interventionist policies that had carried France successfully through the 1950s and the 1960s had not fundamentally changed.

Instead, people began to realize that France's rapid expansion in those earlier years — and indeed its slower progress in the recession years, because although growth slowed down dramatically, it never totally stopped — may have had less to do with government guidelines than with something far more old-fashioned: market forces. Many people would argue that the best thing the state did for French business in the years after 1945 was to get out of its way, by a decision which at the time almost everyone — politicians, civil servants and businessmen alike — thought to be a huge risk: the establishment of the EEC. In fact, it proved to be a huge opportunity for the nation.

The reasons why France took the lead in setting up the European Coal and Steel Community in 1951, and then, in 1957, the EEC, were primarily political. The intention was that Western Europe should be tied together so tightly that a European war could never happen again. On the commercial side, the EEC was to be a common market, with no tariff barriers between member countries. The French people saw it as a trade-off: Their farmers would get new customers for their produce, while German industry would have a sizable, fresh market for its products. Many French industrialists were alarmed at the prospect.

What actually happened was very different. When the Common Market came into effect, customs duties keeping out foreign goods came down. Choice widened, and consumers were no longer virtually forced to buy French. Manufacturers were thereby compelled to produce goods their customers would choose to buy — and in fact those were the kinds of goods that Germans and Italians and Dutchmen wanted too. The spur of competition woke up French industry. The amount spent on imports from EEC countries increased more than tenfold between 1958 and 1972 — but so did the value of French exports. Almost everybody benefited: farmers and industrialists, bosses and workers, producers and consumers alike.

Two other very old-fashioned forces helped to foster the change in attitudes. One was rivalry, the other was greed. French managers and businessmen in the 1950s and 1960s were fascinated by "the American challenge." That phrase was the title of an influential book written by a successful magazine publisher, Jean-Jacques Servan-Schreiber. He was not anti-American, as the Gaullist government was, but he argued that American-based multinational companies were already immensely powerful and they would take control of the European economy, unless — and this was the lesson he wanted to teach — European companies learned to challenge them with their own weapons.

In fact, French business was already learning from the American example. Ambitious managers were studying at Harvard Business School and later at its European imitators, chief among them being INSEAD, Institute Européen d'Administration, or European Institute of Business Administration, a private school in Fontainebleau near Paris, which was established in 1959. They picked up American methods of management and of mass production, and put them into operation. Some also developed the American enthusiasm for opening one's own business. The small French businessman of the 1950s was typically one who, having inherited a business established by his father or grandfather, ran it on much the same lines as they had done before him. Today, he might well be a progressive

Pyramidal apartment buildings and a marina lend a futuristic air to La Grande Motte, one of eight vacation towns built since 1963 by the government between the Rhône delta and the Pyrenees. The resorts were designed to take tourist overflow from the Riviera.

manager who has learned his skills first at a French business school and then as an executive with a multinational firm.

The new lessons were applied to marketing as well as to manufacturing. The immense discount stores — called hypermarchés — that stand on the outskirts of many a French town today, attracting customers with large parking areas and a wide range of goods on display in addition to food, were pioneered in the 1960s by the French firm Carrefour, set up by a one-time small shopkeeper. They created a revolution in French shopping habits, undercutting neighborhood store prices by as much as 20 or even 40 per cent. The biggest of them — garish emporiums that sell everything from bedroom suites, off-the-rack suits and video recorders to packets of salt and frozen foods — outmatch any stores in Europe for size; some have more than 200,000 square feet of floor space and up to 70 check-out counters.

Today, France's businessmen have made American methods their own, and in most fields, including technology, can as easily teach the world as learn from it; only banking and accounting still lag. The principal reason for such frenetic managerial activity lies in an abundance of incentives to succeed. There are few countries where managers eager for the good life can earn the money to afford it more easily than in France. The gap between managers' and workers' pay is high and the workers themselves cannot claim to be badly off. Moreover, the French income tax system has always allowed the well-paid to retain an unusually high proportion of what they earn.

For those who are self-employed, the financial rewards are still higher; for them tax evasion through incomplete

THE GROWTH OF THE NUCLEAR INDUSTRY

France is one of the world leaders in nuclear technology and the reprocessing of irradiated fuels. During Charles de Gaulle's presidency, the French nuclear program was closely linked to the country's defense policy of independent nuclear deterrence, but the oil crisis of the 1970s subsequently spurred developments in the field of energy production for civilian uses: France has little oil but plentiful deposits of uranium.

Although Mitterrand's Socialist government trimmed the nuclear program, nearly 40 per cent of the country's electricity needs were supplied by nuclear power stations by the early 1980s. Opposition has been more muted than in other countries; it is countered by the official view that France has no other way of meeting its energy needs if national independence and living standards are to be maintained.

Two workers at the La Hague nuclear reprocessing plant near Cherbourg prepare a container designed for the transportation of irradiated fuel.

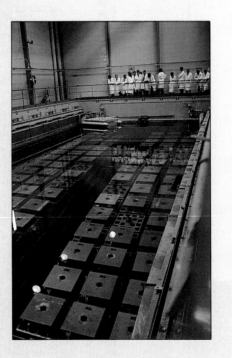

Visitors to the La Hague complex survey flasks of nuclear waste, left to cool for three years under water. The irradiated fuel is then separated into unburned uranium and sent to another plant to be reenriched; plutonium for fast-breeder reactors; and fission products, stored in cement cells.

income returns has long been, and remains, almost a national pastime. The dimensions of fiscal fraud are disturbing; in 1981 a finance minister estimated the amount of money lost to the government to be almost a quarter of the sum paid. Successive administrations have tried to address the problem; but so far none has been able to provide a successful solution.

Besides leading people to reevaluate the reasons for growth, the experience of recession has also inevitably affected the way in which French people look at their working lives. By demonstrating that the locomotive of economic growth can be brought almost to a halt, the years of recession shattered the complacent visions of unlimited progress that once haunted the nation. Yet few people have questioned — as their predecessors in the Depression years of the 1930s did — that it can eventually pick up speed again.

The reason for such optimism is that, despite the problems caused by recession, France's workers — or at least those who still have jobs — continue to live well. Wages are on or slightly above the EEC average, and many employers pay their staff a 13th or even a 14th month's salary, often in the form of a Christmas bonus. Even for the less well-off, the amount of income tax paid is smaller than in most European countries. On the other hand, the burden of value-added tax on purchased commodities is heavy, and it is borne equally by the poor and the rich. The doctor has to be paid and so does the pharamacist, but in both cases some three quarters of the bill will be reimbursed by social security, and many workers subscribe to welfare funds that meet most of the remaining cost. Benefits for

those who are employed can be high, but so are the deductions from paychecks that help to finance them.

Child allowances are generous, and many poorer families receive a housing subsidy. Employees of larger firms may also enjoy extra advantages as a result of the activities of *comités d'entreprise,* elected bodies, presided over by management, that have been obligatory in all companies with more than 50 employees since 1945. Their main function is to improve working conditions, for instance by organizing nurseries, cafeterias, professional training facilities and sometimes even cheap vacations and housing for staff members.

Benefits for working women are particularly favorable, especially in the matter of maternity. Mothers are legally entitled to four months' leave at 90 per cent of their salary for a first or second birth; to encourage couples to have large families, the period is stretched to six months for a third or subsequent child. Mothers and fathers also have the option of taking an unpaid year off work after the birth of a child with the guarantee of their job back afterward; for companies with

99

SUBTERRANEAN TREASURES

Though hardly the most obvious of France's culinary resources, cellars have long played an honorable part in the preparation of the nation's gourmet foodstuffs. Their best-known use, at least since Roman times, has been for storing wine. Even with heat-controlled storage containers available, producers of champagne and other fine wines still consider their subterranean depots — carved in the Champagne area from the chalky substrata — one of their greatest natural assets.

The constant temperature and humidity that make cellars ideal for aging wine are also ideal for growing mushrooms, cultivated in the Ile de France and other regions in man-made underground corridors. Cheesemakers of Roquefort, in the Massif Central, use the natural limestone caves to produce sheep's cheese. Microorganisms, found in the caverns, are injected into the product to create its blue veining.

Mushroom farmers wearing miners' lamps gather their crop in a Provençal cellar.

Champagne bottles are rotated to allow sediment to settle.

Roquefort cheese matures in a cool limestone cavern.

more than 100 employees, the period is two years. Nursery schools, or child-care centers provided by employers, are more common than in most European countries.

For the ambitious, educated woman, the barriers to success in a career are far lower nowadays than they used to be. Many girls — almost as many as boys — go on from elementary school to higher education. As a result, more women are to be found in, or at least rising toward, high positions in the professions or in business than in the past. But farther down the scale, women remain less than equal. They may get equal pay for equal work, but somehow the lower-paid jobs turn out to be mainly women's jobs. This may well change as brain replaces brawn as a way of earning a living in modern society. But for the time being, in a country where the distance between the top of the heap and the bottom is wide, most women are still fairly near the bottom.

The real bottom of France's heap, however, is not French at all. It is made up of the immigrant workers who have taken over jobs that Frenchmen no longer want to do. These immigrants came flooding in during the boom years, from Portugal, Spain, Italy and North and Central Africa. By the mid-1970s, France had about four million immigrants, with about 1.75 million at work, around one in 12 of the total working population.

The inflow was welcomed and encouraged during the years when labor was short. The building industry, for instance, depended heavily on foreigners. In many tedious, dangerous or dirty-workplaces — for example, car assembly lines and some textile factories — they even formed a majority of the work force. But the new arrivals also brought problems. They generally got the worst housing, as well as the worst jobs. Only a few remnants survive of the *bidonvilles* — shanty towns built of flattened tin cans — where the North Africans originally squatted. But a majority are still housed in low-cost housing, sometimes in what are virtually Arab ghettoes.

Of the immigrants, the Algerians who flooded into France after the end of their war of independence have faced the greatest hostility and the greatest difficulties. Unlike the European immigrants, who often came to France with their families, the Algerians tended, at least in the early days of immigration, to be young men on their own. Their position was made worse by the fact that they were seldom union-ized, and often did not dare to be, for many had arrived illegally and knew that any trouble with their boss could mean that they would be denounced and packed off home to Algeria.

Like so many other problems, the question of immigration was worsened by the recession, with the growth of a feeling, particularly among the working class, that the immigrants were in competition for jobs that were suddenly scarce. Worried by an increase in racial assaults, politicians of all parties agreed that an improvement in the economic climate would undoubtedly lessen the tension.

But the problems of the economy itself seemed equally intractable. One cause for concern was a rapid growth of imports that was no longer balanced, as in earlier years, by a comparable surge in export sales. In 1970, France bought 26 per cent of the capital goods that it needed, such as machinery, from abroad. By 1981, the figure had risen to 48 per cent. For motor vehicles the percentage of imports was up from 18 to 32 per cent, for textiles and clothing from 12 to 37 per cent, for shoes from 13 to 43 per cent. Not surprisingly, many people argued that the way to re-capture the home market for home industry was simply to block out as many imports as possible.

But there were other voices also to point out that that route had already been tried, and that it had led to the long sleep from which the French economy only awakened after World War II. Advocates of this view argued that protectionism was the root cause of the stagnation and apathy of the 1930s, and that the answer to the problems of recession lay elsewhere. They stressed that the key to France's improved future lay in the money that was being poured into training and retraining in modern skills, and into research and development in key modern techniques and industries. They also recognized a crucial fact about the French economy today: Industry only employs about 35 per cent of those who work. Service jobs, on the other hand, provide work for 55 per cent, as bank employees, teachers, computer programmers, hotel employees and the like. Consequently, any policy that served the short-term interests of industry at the expense of the economy as a whole would be unacceptable.

By general consensus, little is predictable about the direction the French economy will take in the years to come except that it can never revert to what it was before the last world war. A future of heavy industry protected by high tariff walls is no more probable than a return to the still older, agricultural ways, the peasant past that France has now left behind. □

A SHOWPLACE OF CHIC

Photographs by Kevin Kling

Ever since Louis XIV's mercantilist chief minister Colbert decided to encourage the development of the luxury trades, France has been renowned as a retail center for all the accoutrements of elegant living. Nowhere is that reputation more richly earned than in the Faubourg St. Honoré quarter of Paris. From Laroche and Yves St. Laurent to Cardin and Courrèges, the names of its great couturiers are a litany of luxury that attracts a clientele of the rich and famous from around the world.

The quarter's principal artery, the rue du Faubourg St. Honoré, was in the 18th Century a street of town houses for the aristocracy, and many of the businesses now occupying its buildings have retained the atmosphere of exclusive private residences. A few disdain to show their wares in anything so mundane as a shop window. But the majority of them have turned storefront display into a fine art, so that Paris' *haute couture* center is also a delight for those who can only afford to look.

Signaled by a white-on-blue enamel street sign of a kind found throughout the capital *(right)*, Paris' rue du Faubourg St. Honoré shelters many of the best-known fashion houses — among them Lanvin, whose display of spring outfits attracts two passers-by on a rainy winter day *(above)*.

Chandeliers and 18th Century paneling decorate Cartier the jewelers in the rue de la Paix.

A stylish trio lingers outside a shop that sells children's clothes.

A boutique adjoins a ministry building.

Windows advertise a hairdressing salon in a courtyard off the Faubourg St. Honoré.

Luxury leather goods gleam among marbled columns in the window of Hermès, which has occupied the same corner site for more than a century.

In the late afternoon, customers have refreshments at Ladurée, a tea salon and patisserie in the rue Royale.

At Fauchon, a specialist food store in the Place de la Madeleine, a salesman advises a customer.

A well-heeled couple leaves the Hotel Meurice on the rue de Rivoli.

A well-to-do family enjoys an alfresco lunch on the grounds of their château in the Beaujolais region. Leisurely lunches at home — once a hallowed tradition — are enjoyed whenever possible. But with more people commuting to work, the practice has been largely abandoned in the cities.

A PASSION FOR GOOD LIVING

The traditional image of the good life in France fits uneasily with the economic revolution of the postwar years. Its pleasures — leisurely, conservative, often rural — have little in common with the hurried urban lifestyle typical of the new affluence. The changes wrought by prosperity have affected, for better or for worse, almost every aspect of the way in which people spend their spare time, from the places where they shop — discount stores are replacing the old corner grocery stores — to the way in which they spend their evenings, now often passed in front of the television set when once they might have been whiled away in a café.

The transitional state of France today, halfway between a harsh peasant past that still exerts a strong nostalgic pull and a future of technological conveniences and spiritual uncertainties, can be seen in the look of the land, or at least its inhabited portions. Imagine, if you will, a typical village, somewhere just south of the line below which the red tiles of the south replace the gray slate roofing of the north. The buildings usually focus on a small, central square, shaded with plane or chestnut trees, with maybe an old, mossy fountain playing in the middle. On one side of the square stands the village church, probably several centuries old, and on the other side the *mairie* (town hall), a sedate 19th Century pile with a flight of stone steps in front and a flagpole where the red, white and blue tricolor flies on special days. Nearby is a war memorial, bearing the names of those killed in World War I — a long list —

and World War II (fewer, but including Resistance fighters shot by the Germans, or deportees who died in German camps), as well as the victims of more recent colonial wars. All around are small, traditional shops: a butcher's, a *boulangerie* providing crisp bread freshly baked each day, and also a small supermarket and a smart new boutique selling jewelry and stylish dresses, signs of the postwar spread of prosperity from the cities to rural areas.

The village remains a tight-knit community, a protective but gossipy world where everyone pries into everyone else's life. The main centers of social life are the cafés, where men gather to play cards or to argue over glasses of red wine. On fine evenings, some will desert the café for a side square to play *pétanque* or *boules,* a quintessentially French version of bowling played with metal balls on a flat piece of ground. The village then goes to bed early; but much later, at midnight, its peace may be shattered by the roar of motorcycles bringing the local youths and their girlfriends back from some nearby discotheque. Such is local life, a blend of the old and the new.

Provincial cities, too, mix modernism with tradition. Dijon, Angers, Nancy, Montpellier — these and a hundred other graceful old cities, large and small, have changed a lot since prewar days. They used to be dignified but lethargic, lovely to visit but often dull to live in. Now they have mushroomed in size and many of them pulsate with new activity. They are ringed with suburban housing tracts, and their main streets

and boulevards are congested with traffic. Perhaps this has spoiled some of their charm, but for the inhabitants the growth has meant better stores and a fuller and more varied cultural and social life. Most of these towns have an old, historic quarter, usually found off the main streets, near the castle or the cathedral; this area will have been tastefully preserved and maybe partially closed to traffic — and here all the grace and beauty of the ancient days live on, coexisting with the modern, downtown hubbub.

The changes extend from the street into the home. The French, who often used to frequent cafés in order to escape cramped and ill-provided apartments, are now better housed and spend more time and money on their living quarters. They have even come to enjoy the pastime of do-it-yourself home maintenance, which used to interest them little. With the spread of suburban homes, they have become avid gardeners, too; on exit roads outside many towns, garden centers now do a busy trade.

Leisure activities of all kinds are on the increase, because people have more spare time than ever before. Since World War II, workers have shown a preference for extending weekends and annual vacations rather than shortening daily working hours. Executives may often stay at their desks until 7 or 8 p.m.; but even for them *le weekend* has become sacred — a far cry from the not-so-distant days when the work week extended into Saturday and no word for the end of the week even existed, there-

5

by necessitating the borrowing of the English term. For city-dwellers in particular, the two-day break, with its promise of escape from stress and the chance to get away to a country retreat, has become an essential release valve.

The second home has become a cult, especially for Parisians used to living in cramped apartments. Often it is an old family dwelling, inherited from ancestors who lived and worked there in the rural past. Otherwise it may be an old farmstead bought cheap and modernized, or a fashionable new villa or a seaside condo. Whatever it is, its owner will cheerfully brave the traffic jams on Friday and Sunday nights, sometimes even driving hundreds of miles to attain his weekend rural idyll. France holds the world record for ownership of these properties; one family in nine owns one, as against one in 15 in the United States, one in 140 in West Germany and one in 200 in Britain.

Often owners of such properties will be prepared to sacrifice much of their other social life to be able to enjoy their second home to the full. As one owner, a 34-year-old technician from Lyon, puts it: "We have a small downtown apartment in an area that is almost as noisy and hectic as Paris. Every Friday, with my wife and two kids, I take the three-hour drive to the old Auvergne farmhouse I inherited from my grandfather. There we go swimming in the river and riding, we chat with the local people, my wife makes jam from the fruit in our orchard, and I do carpentry. We feel alive! I don't think I could stand my city job without this release, so I'm quite happy to have no evening social life in Lyon during the week."

Annual vacations are seized upon with equal enthusiasm. Before the war, these were largely the preserve of the well-to-do; now, French wage earners have won themselves a legal minimum of five weeks' vacation, a longer paid leave than in most countries in Europe. Some will spend most or all of it at their place in the country; most of the remaining will pass the time crowding France's many beaches. The crush is exacerbated by a marked unwillingness to stagger the vacation time: For most people it is high summer or nothing. For a month and a half, from mid-July to the end of August, most cities become ghost towns, while the beaches are lined with pink flesh turning tan and holiday traffic raises the accident rate from its normal high level to a horrific summer peak.

Others have more exotic tastes; active and adventurous vacations are on the increase, and so is foreign travel. From time to time, the government imposes currency restrictions to lessen the outflow of French capital; when these are not in force, however, one vacation in four is taken abroad. Spain is by far the most popular destination, but a surprising number of overseas trips are to far-distant locales — backpacking treks in Nepal, for instance, or tours of the monuments of ancient Peru.

Back home, camping attracts about six million people every year, though few of these vacationers are interested in the wilderness life. Instead, they congregate on enormous, well-organized sites, like armies mobilized for leisure. Along less built-up western stretches of the Riviera, canvas cities of gaudy blue and orange tents fill the pine forests for miles. Along the length of the Mediterranean coast, customs have changed radically since the war. The trend has been away from the Edwardian sedateness of Nice or Monte Carlo and toward the slick and sensual sophistication of

The Countess of Saint-Seine exercises some of the greyhounds that she breeds at her château in the Touraine district. Burdened by a wealth tax imposed in 1981, many of the landed aristocracy have had to sell their châteaux or open their doors to the paying public.

St. Tropez. Among the young, the bathing suit has all but disappeared, and the bikini too is threatened. Almost all the beaches are topless today, and bare breasts are also to be seen in some seafront stores and cafés. Total nudism is accepted in certain locations; indeed, at Cap d'Agde on the Languedoc coast is Europe's largest nudist resort, with room for 20,000 visitors.

It is a curiously French paradox that a people so individualistic — and, when they get the chance, so closely territorial — can be so cheerfully gregarious during vacation. Formality goes by the board, and everyone seems to find a therapeutic pleasure in ignoring the rules of everyday life back home. The flamboyant success of the Club Méditerranée is a case in point. At scores of club "villages," no longer restricted to the Mediterranean coast but scattered worldwide, jaded city-dwellers escape their workaday selves to play the noble savage, wearing vaguely Tahitian costumes and using beads for money. In the purest Club Méditerranée resorts, they will enjoy the back-to-nature pleasures of bare straw huts with no electric lights or plumbing. Of course, they have to pay money for the beads in the first place, but only at the bar; the Club offers good food, free wine at meals, extensive sports facilities, a distinctly sexy ambience and, above all, a remarkable camaraderie that the French often find hard to attain in the stratified society back home.

Others find a kind of camaraderie in sports. Spectator events are widely popular, especially soccer matches and the annual Tour de France bicycle race. But the greatest increase has been in individual participation. For some, this may mean nothing more energetic than a quiet game of *boules* in a city park; for others, though, it is a more energetic affair altogether. One example is Yves Gonnsard, a 38-year-old advertising executive from Grenoble, who claims: "I'm passionate about various kinds of sports — to keep fit, yes, but also because I enjoy the competition. That's very French — we're a highly competitive people. Whatever I do — tennis, sailing, skiing — I play to win. It's no fun otherwise."

More than four million French men and women go to the ski slopes every year. Some to the Pyrenees, the Vosges in eastern France or the Massif Central, but most to the French Alps. Hotel owners there recount anecdotes of ski-mad clients who will drive 360 miles from Paris through the night for a mere weekend's sport. Sailing is also booming; the number of private boats has risen from 20,000 in 1960 to almost half a million today. Hunting of wild game, though still widespread, is on the wane, but fishing and tennis are more popular than ever. So too is horseback riding; membership in riding clubs increased tenfold in the 1970s. Team sports are most popular in France in two forms: Soccer attracts almost one and a half million regular players, while an estimated 170,000 play rugby. In their own hometowns, people have more scope than in the past for practicing sports in the evenings and on weekends, thanks to the construction of new gymnasiums and swimming pools.

No other leisure activity, however, is enjoyed with such universal relish and gusto as savoring food. The French countryside provides a rich and varied crop of comestibles, and its abundance is matched by the energy and care with which the nation's cooks put it to use. Add to that basic combination the per-

A peasant farmhouse in the depopulated Auvergne region represents the kind of rural idyll that is the dream of many a French city-dweller. One in nine French families owns a second home — a higher proportion than any other Western European nation.

THE UNHURRIED PLEASURES OF BOULES

One of the best-loved of French pastimes, especially in the south, is the game of *boules,* an informal version of bowling. The requirements are simple: a flat piece of ground — often a town or village square well served with cafés; a sufficient number of players to make the event a social as well as a sports event; and the shiny, cast-iron balls themselves.

The game is usually played by two teams of two or three players with three balls each. One of the contestants throws a small, wooden ball called the *cochonnet* — "little pig" — to a distance of between 16 and 30 feet. Players from each team then take it in turn to pitch their balls, aiming to get as close to the *cochonnet* as possible or else to knock their opponents' balls away.

When all the balls have been thrown, the team with the ball nearest to the *cochonnet* is the winner. It scores one point for that ball, and an extra point for each additional one closer to the *cochonnet* than the nearest of their opponents'. A game goes to 13 or 15 points, and a match typically consists of three games.

Dotted across the scene like figures in a Brueghel landscape, *boules* enthusiasts practice their sport in a St. Tropez square.

A player delivers a ball from the obligatory stationary position.

A player measures the distance from ball to *cochonnet*.

vasive national flair for the good things in life and complete the mixture with a certain high seriousness of purpose of a very Gallic kind. The result is the finest cooking in the world. Of all the arts of living, the art of eating well is the most archetypically French.

La cuisine française did not come into being overnight. Up until the Middle Ages, Frenchmen ate much the way they had done since the time of the Gauls, whose idea of a banquet was a mighty table loaded up with ox, venison, wild boar, bear, game birds, hares, capons, pikes and a comprehensive selection of every other foodstuff available. The meat was roasted or boiled, or sometimes even armor-plated with a casing of crude pastry. In any case, quantity took priority over quality, since the meal's purpose was less to charm the palates of the guests than to glut them into insensibility.

Historians have traced the origins of the transformation of French cooking to the year 1533, when Catherine de Medici married the future King Henry II. She was only 14 at the time, but already she was a noted gourmet and she saw no reason why she should endure permanent indigestion as well as homesickness for her native Italy. The skilled chefs she brought with her in her entourage transformed the French court's attitude to food, and laid the foundations of an art her adoptive people soon made their own.

In the following century, aristocrats and wealthy merchants vied with each other for the services of the growing number of *maîtres de cuisine*. The culinary profession also acquired its first martyr when, in 1671, Vatel, chef to the prince of Condé, failed to provide sufficient fish for a banquet for the king of France. Vatel knew where his duty lay.

5

Diners crowd a *relais routier* restaurant — one of a network of eating-places, each identified by a distinctive red and blue sign, that cater to truck drivers and other road users. Regularly checked for quality by inspectors, they have a reputation for wholesome, inexpensive food.

Distraught, he retired to his chamber and fell upon his sword.

Curiously, the first restaurant did not open until 1765. The word, which has passed into most of the world's languages, comes from the "restorative" qualities of the soup its owner sold; to this day, the great chefs of France describe themselves ironically as "soup merchants." (But only among themselves; outsiders would be well advised to choose a more respectful term.) The idea was already well established when the Revolution of 1789 came to trouble the climate of gastronomic well-being with a new mood of spartan austerity. "If it had lasted," the gastronome Grimaud de la Reynière wrote with a shudder, "France might have lost the recipe for chicken *fricassée*."

In the long run, however, the Revolution actually widened the clientele for good eating. Private chefs, thrown out of work by the exile or execution of their patrons, needed a fresh outlet for their skills, and found plenty of well-heeled Republican customers. The 19th Century saw gastronomy reach unprecedented heights. Under Talleyrand, foreign minister to Napoleon and his successors, it became an instrument of government policy; banquets created by his master-chef Marie-Antoine Carême were designed as surely as Talleyrand's speeches to seduce foreign ambassadors into serving the interests of French diplomacy.

Carême himself cared nothing about politics: He was a conceited, arrogant man but he was also a culinary genius, and he took advantage of the unlimited budgets and huge kitchen staffs provided for him to invent the style of food that came to be known as *haute cuisine* — high cooking. Appropriately, he also invented the *toque* — the high, white hat

that has ever since been the badge of office of the chef.

Haute cuisine, as devised by the grandiose Carême and developed by his enthusiastic acolytes, is elaborate and expensive, both in terms of the ingredients used and the efforts devoted to preparing them. Rich meats, as often as not studded with truffles, are served with even richer sauces — ranging from intensely flavored meaty reductions, to voluptuous coatings of eggs and cream.

It is formal, often ostentatiously so, and it is not, perhaps, the healthiest diet, yet in the hands of its greatest practitioners, men like Auguste Escoffier who, as the associate of the hotelier César Ritz, carried the gospel of French cuisine around Europe in the *belle époque,* it was and can be a cuisine of the greatest imaginable finesse.

But it is a style of cooking that is out of place in the bustling France of today. The 19th Century writer and gourmet,

Charles-Augustin Sainte-Beuve, could pat his stately belly without remorse and say, "Rejoice, my little stomach, all that I earn is yours." A modern Frenchman, though, is more likely to be worried about his waistline. In France, as elsewhere in the world, rich foods are going out of fashion.

Good food, though, has never been more in fashion; since the 1960s, a much-publicized *nouvelle cuisine* — new cooking — has emerged to supplant the

5

older style and rescue the nation from obesity and indigestion. It does nothing, however, to help the state of its devotees' bank balances, for just as much as *haute cuisine*, it uses expensive ingredients. It prepares them in a lighter, supposedly purer style, however, and avoids the heavy sauces of the past, which sometimes masked all subtlety of taste. Food is cooked rapidly in its own juices, almost in the Chinese way. Flavors are daringly blended: steamed oysters on a bed of leeks or chicken with raspberry vinegar. The chef's greatest asset is no longer his knowledge of tradition but his imagination.

The new approach to cooking was pioneered by a few patron-chefs of undoubted genius — Paul Bocuse, the Troisgros brothers, Michel Guérard and others — who quickly became star names both at home and abroad. Under their expert leadership, *nouvelle cuisine* caught on so widely in sophisticated circles that could afford it that by the late 1970s nearly three quarters of France's most highly rated restaurants had adopted the new style of cooking. Inevitably, the license to invent recipes led to unpalatable abuses, as young chefs eager for fame and fortune began to offer the public such horrors as raw sweetbreads. Their excesses gave *nouvelle cuisine* a bad name.

Today, the vogue has passed its prime and *nouvelle cuisine* is merging back into the tradition from which it sprang. In a sense, it had never really left it; for as its pioneers point out, it is less of a break with the past than a return to the true spirit of French country cooking, in which everything should taste of itself as it is.

Yet the excitement and controversy that the coming of *nouvelle cuisine* provoked has shown that gastronomy can still arouse great passions — scarcely to be wondered at in a land where great chefs are national celebrities and the subject of food is one to which a substantial fraction of the country's publishing industry is dedicated. The most established and the oldest of the great food guides is the *Michelin*. Though its

influence has declined somewhat of late, its world-famous award of one, two or three stars to France's best restaurants is still awaited annually with fascination (and, in some circles, with apprehension: In the 1960s, one chef reacted to downgrading by shooting himself). Nowadays, the most lively of the guides is produced by the journalistic partnership of Henri Gault and Christian Millau, the men who coined the phrase *nouvelle cuisine*. Gault-Millau (they welded themselves for business purposes into a single national institution) also publish a popular monthly food magazine, but it is the appearance of their guide with the annual rundown on the nation's eating places that has the gourmets lining up in the streets.

Interest in good eating is as marked as ever, then, but there are contradictory factors counterbalancing the trend. Convenience foods, to which the French put up a lengthy resistance, have at last begun to make serious inroads. *Le fast food,* it is called, sometimes with bitterness as if to imply there is an American plot; but it is, alas, the French who are paying to eat *les hotdogs* and *les hamburgers* dispensed by city snack bars in increasing numbers. At home, too, eating habits are changing. Although the French in the 1980s consume only one third as much frozen food as their neighbors in Britain and Germany, they are catching up at a rate that may delight *le marketingman* but would have broken Escoffier's heart.

Eating well is not under threat, for it is too deeply ingrained in the French character. Certainly, it is not the property of any particular social class. Some of the best simple cooking in France is to be found in the *relais routiers,* truck stops, used by the nation's truck drivers; and although the pressures of industrial life have encouraged people to stay at work to eat the noon meal rather than to go home — 60 per cent of the work force in the Paris region now take their meals in cafeterias — trade unions and works councils make sure that the food served in them is of a quality that would be unheard of in other nations.

On a cobbled square, the people of Villefranche-de-Rouergue in southwestern France trade news and produce. Most towns and large villages have such open-air markets, where food, household goods, and other items are sold cheaper than in the stores.

The window of a *charcuterie* advertises some of the culinary delights within, among them smoked salmon, sausage and snails in butter. Originally cooked-meat stores, *charcuteries* still specialize in pork dishes such as sausages, hams, pâtés and local or regional preparations.

DIGGING FOR THE DIAMONDS OF COOKERY

Praised in poetry and eulogized by gourmets the world over, truffles are one of France's most prestigious and expensive foods. With good reason, the culinary writer Anthelme Brillat-Savarin called these odoriferous black fungi "the diamonds of cookery."

Mentioned in recipes from the days of imperial Rome, truffles are now found mainly in areas of southwestern France, where they make an important contribution to the local economy. A certain amount of mystery surrounds their growth, and attempts to cultivate them artificially have had at best a limited success. They flourish in poor limestone soil lightly planted with trees, especially oaks, near whose roots they form.

Truffles grow as deep as 12 inches below ground, so finding them calls for special skills. While some truffle hunters can locate their prize by sighting telltale columns of flies that live on the fungi, they are usually traced by their smell. A few individuals have sufficiently fine noses to track them down unaided, but most hunters rely on the scenting abilities of a trained pig or dog.

Ranging in size from the span of an acorn to the bulk of a grapefruit, the truffles are sorted out for market and sold either fresh or canned, whole or in slivers. Since good specimens are in strong demand, poaching is rife, and damaged or broken fungi may be stuck together with toothpicks so as to command higher prices.

A pig trained to hunt for truffles roots along the ground while its owner keeps a firm hold on its leash, ready to distract the animal with corn once it uncovers the precious quarry. Dogs are now more widely used than pigs, because they do not eat the prize.

Truffle gatherers wait with their crop for trading to begin at a market in Lalbenque in southwestern France *(left)*. Having examined the specimens closely — sometimes a magnifying glass is used — a dealer hands a promissory note of payment to a seller whose offerings he has favored.

5

In any case, away from the bustle of the cities, traditional ways have changed far less and the old order often still endures. Anyone who doubts it need only pay a visit to a small French country town between the hours of noon and 3 p.m. There is a reverential quality about the silence that descends upon the place. The streets are deserted, the stores shuttered, the houses radiate an aura of transcendental peace. A Martian anthropologist, climbing down from his spaceship, might easily conclude that he had come upon the natives at a time of worship. And in a way he would be right: The townspeople are having lunch.

France without good food would scarcely be France at all; and good food in France implies good wine to accompany it. Wine puts in an appearance at almost every table in the land, from the cheap jug of *gros rouge,* crude red, in a workman's café to the exalted vintages of Burgundy and Bordeaux that grace a gourmet's banquet. It is the lifeblood of the nation. In a good year, France expects to produce some 10 billion bottles — a quarter of the world's output. Only about 4 per cent of production is destined for export. Some, of course, goes to be distilled; but most of it is swallowed by the thirsty French, in quantities that average out to more than 23 gallons a year for every man, woman and child.

The produce is graded and classified by strict governmental controls. French wine laws are the oldest and most thoroughgoing in the world. The most highly rated wines are granted the right to call themselves *Appellation Contrôlée,* or controlled nomenclature; the next grade is made up of the *Vins Délimités de Qualité Supérieure,* higher quality wines

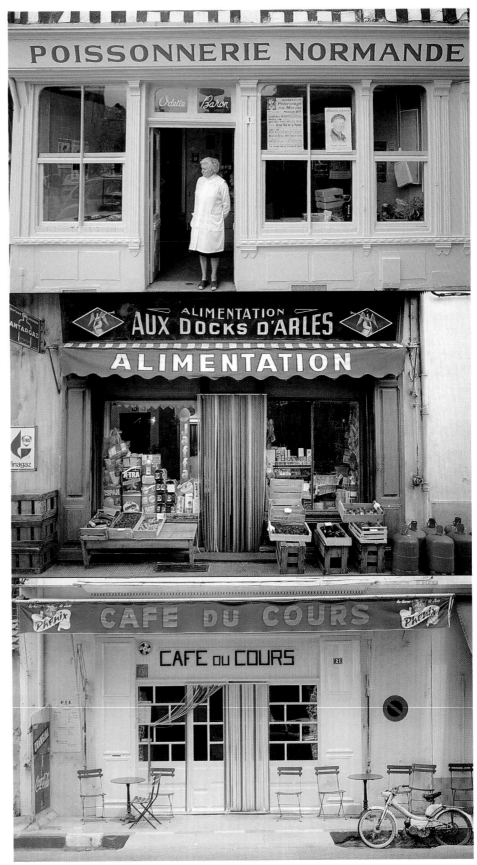

A fish market in Normandy, a grocery store in Arles and a café in the south exemplify the small traditional retail outlet. Since the 1950s, many of these family businesses have vanished, outpriced by discount stores that have sprung up near most towns.

often referred to acronymically as VDQS. Then come the simpler *Vins de Pays* — regional wines with a regional character. The lowest in the classification rank are sold as *Vins de Table*, table wines which may be anonymous blends but are still subjected to government quality control. Outside this four-part classification system are the *Vins Ordinaires*, which are labeled by their alcohol content.

Exported wines tend to belong to one of the two higher categories. The others — the unsung majority — rarely leave France. They only cost a few francs a bottle — often less than the cost of a bottle of mineral water. In recent years, however, they have been experiencing strong competition from the Italian and Spanish vineyards; some 800 million or so additional bottles are imported every year. Consequently, Paris bureaucrats and canny viticulturists have realized that, in an affluent but competitive world, it makes sense to move up-market and to concentrate on quality rather than quantity. Government money is available for winegrowers who choose to improve their product by uprooting poor vines and replacing them with finer stock. As a result, the percentage of *Appellation Contrôlée* and VDQS wine has been increasing steadily.

Wine sales as a whole in France have been declining over the past few years, largely as a result of the smaller amount of cheap wine consumed. As if in counterpoint, however, home sales of spirits have been increasing. The aristocrat of French spirits is Cognac, the brandy produced in and around the town of that name north of Bordeaux. Cognac also has an immense export market, which has helped to provide the hard cash required to increase yields four-

fold since the 1960s. The brandies of Armagnac, 120 miles to the south, can be every bit as good as those of Cognac; but the district's many small-scale producers usually lack the capital to finance the lengthy aging required to satisfy the most demanding of palates. Many other winegrowing districts also make their own brandies, often very good clear spirits, known as *eaux-de-vie de marc,* but none has so far succeeded in making much of an international reputation for itself.

Not all French spirits originate with the grape. The apples of Normandy — and parts of Brittany — yield *calvados,* a fine and fiery drink that can mature with time into something approaching the quality of Cognac. From Alsace comes the delicious white plum-brandy known as *mirabelle.* And in much of the South of France the staple local liquor is *pastis.* Flavored with aniseed or licorice,

it is drunk diluted with ice and water as a cool aperitif for a hot day. Nowadays, though, the most popular spirit in France is not French at all. The sales of Scotch whisky quadrupled in France during the 1970s, and it is now the most widely drunk aperitif, at least among the middle class.

All this happy tippling has its darker side, however. The French are among the heaviest drinkers in the world, averaging the equivalent of 3.9 gallons of pure alcohol each in 1980. Comparable figures for that year were 3.3 gallons per capita in West Germany, 2.3 in the United States and 1.9 in Britain. The effects on the national health are depressingly predictable. Nearly 20,000 people die every year from alcohol-induced conditions, notably cirrhosis of the liver; only heart disease and cancer — themselves sometimes related to alcohol — are bigger killers.

MIGRATING TO THE SUN

One of the most extraordinary spectacles in France is the annual summer pilgrimage to the coast. Almost half of all vacations are spent by the sea, and since most people take their vacations in July and August, the result is traffic congestion on the roads, the collapse of services in the deserted cities and a corresponding overloading of resort facilities.

But the vacationers love it. For three or four weeks, they sunbathe and swim, eat and drink, put on weight and take off clothes, make friends, make sandcastles or do nothing. Then it is time to join the traffic jam homeward, leaving many hotels struggling for business until next year's invasion.

Despite government efforts to stagger vacations, the French still take 80 per cent of their vacations between July 14 and August 31. But with more annual leave than most people in Europe, they also find time for breaks at other periods of the year.

122

5

Forty per cent of hospital patients evince some symptoms of alcoholism; and two thirds of France's mentally handicapped children are born of alcoholic parents. The problem comes less from Scotch and other fashionable drinks than from heavy consumption of coarse red wine and cheap *eau-de-vie*. Oddly enough, the situation is most serious not in the wine-growing south, but in Brittany and the industrial Nord department, where no vines grow but plenty of cheap wine is imported. Many Bretons drink more than one gallon of red wine a day.

Serious as they are, these figures are an improvement on the situation in the 1960s, when alcohol consumption ran as high as 7.3 gallons for every adult in the population. Successive administrations have made strenuous efforts, by way of publicity campaigns, to discourage heavy drinking. With increasing prosperity, people have in any case been shifting away from massive consumption of rough, inexpensive wines toward smaller quantities of better-quality wines and spirits. The amount of money they spend may have stayed the same, but the damage to hearts and livers has diminished.

In France too, as in many countries in the Western world, a rising interest in health matters encourages many people, especially the young, to keep clear of heavy drinking. Sales of fruit juices and mineral waters have tripled, despite their relatively high cost. A 24-year-old secretary from the city of Nancy sums up the new attitudes: "When I meet my friends in a café after work, we usually have colas or mineral water, but rarely aperitifs. We'd drink far more fruit juice than we do if it didn't cost twice as much as cheap wine—it's absurd. I go home for lunch, where my parents still drink wine, but I have a glass of milk. It's healthier."

Material pleasures apart, there is a darker side to the France of affluence and leisure, reflecting the psychological stresses imposed on any people forced to adapt to new conditions, however agreeable in themselves those conditions may be. In the early postwar years, France urbanized very rapidly, maybe too rapidly for its own good. Cities doubled or tripled in size as millions migrated from the land, and ex-peasants found themselves having to cope with the new strains of big-city living. Many millions of people have been rehoused since the war in new suburbs, where certainly they live far more comfortably than in their old slums and peasant farmsteads. And yet they have not always found the accompanying change in lifestyle easy to accommodate. For them, a prosperity bought at the cost of noisy, congested cities and lives spent bowed head down into the winds of competition has been bought too dearly.

Inevitably, a reaction set in. In the 1960s and 1970s in France, as elsewhere in the Western world, a concern for ecology became fashionable. For many, this meant no more than the addition of a new theme to the repertoire of subjects for debate in the café or at the dinner table. For others, it meant a real compulsion to search out their own rural roots—and in France, for historical reasons, those roots are both deeper and more easily accessible than in most other countries.

For many, the urge could be satisfied by buying a weekend cottage or taking long excursions into the country; for others, though, it meant a more permanent return to their own origins in a France where regional attachments remain strong. Usually it has not been a matter of going back to the farms, for good agricultural land is hard to come by, but to small factories or offices near the ancestral home. And sometimes a new start is more important than a return: There are Paris-born executives, for example, tired of the big-city ratrace, who go off with a sense of mission to start up a tiny company in some corner of rural France that they had never heard of before.

More radical still are the sentiments of some young city intellectuals, who choose to abandon all prospects of a conventional career and try their hand at hill-farming in poor upland areas like the Cévennes. Prompted in many cases by the ideals of the 1968 student revolt, they have opted for a "purer" life of stark simplicity, scratching a living from a kitchen garden, small-scale agriculture or stock-raising—breeding goats on a few stony square miles, perhaps—or from handicrafts they can sell to summer visitors.

Les marginaux, they are called, the marginals; the name is appropriate, for not only are they living on the fringes of French society, but their own existence is marginal. Many of the *marginaux* have failed and returned defeated to the cities. Others, though, are more determined to succeed and seem to be staying in the countryside. One such, called Jean-Luc, used to be a Lyon schoolteacher. Now, toughened by hard work and harder winters high in the Massif Central, he sits comfortably on the wiry pony he uses for transport, an austere figure fitting naturally into a rugged landscape. "When I worked in the system, I didn't know who I was. I'm still not sure what I should call myself. A renegade intellectual? A hippie? A peasant? Maybe, maybe not. But I'll tell you this. I know I'm me."

The *marginaux* are few and their direct influence is very small. But France in general has become very aware of environmental values, and "quality of life" has become something of a catch phrase. The concern for this elusive factor can be seen in the determined restoration of old buildings and the creation of neatly paved traffic-free zones in old city centers, in the revival of regional cultures and in the proliferation of local arts festivals. It is manifest in a passionate new concern for history, especially of the local variety — an interest that carried *Montaillou,* Emmanuel Le Roy Ladurie's scholarly account of medieval life in a Cathar village in the Pyrenees, to sales of well over a million copies. It can be found too in the search for private satisfactions, enjoyed in the company of select groups of friends or of local community groups. The growing interest in music, in sports and in serious cuisine are all signs of this new form of restrained hedonism.

It remains to be seen whether the effects of this trend will be positive or negative. What is already apparent is the need for a new direction after 30 years of growth, and a redefinition of the terms on which the good life can be sought in France. The signposts are pointing toward a gentler model of society, less hectically ambitious than in the postwar years, with greater emphasis on local self-help, the importance of human sympathy and support of a neighborly community. In the words of a middle-aged commuter from a village on the outskirts of Paris: "People have come to realize that life is not so long and work is not after all the center of everything. Maybe we are discovering again what *joie de vivre* means." □

A Sunday hunter shoulders his gun after a day's sport near Bordeaux. Shooting is a major leisure activity in France. In 1980, there were 2 million licensed hunters — the highest per capita rate in Western Europe.

THE FAMILY UNIT

Serpentine blocks of low-rent apartments form the estate of La Grande Borne at Grigny, 15 miles south of Paris. The complex, which accommodates 15,000 people, is one of several housing projects built in the past two decades to reduce Paris' severe overcrowding.

In the past, the pattern of authority within French homes was closely defined. Power was vested in the father, a patriarchal figure commanding obedience. The *Code Napoléon,* the civil code enacted in 1804, gave husbands the right to dispose of their wives' property, to prohibit them from working and even to open their mail; and their rights as parents over their offspring were equally absolute. These and similar provisions were reformed in a piecemeal way over the following century, but not until 1942, under legislation passed by the Vichy government, was the principle of equal rights within a marriage enshrined in law. Even then, women had to wait for the Matrimonial Act of 1964 to be able to open a bank account, run a shop or get a passport without their husbands' permission.

Today the situation is very different. The family is still the principal unit of social life, but with the new freedoms and affluence acquired since World War II, attitudes toward it and within it have significantly changed.

To begin with, the family has partly lost the spiritual prop of the Catholic Church. The decline in churchgoing has been dramatic. Although 86 per cent of the population is baptized into the Church, only 14 per cent now regularly attends Mass. In just 15 years up to 1980, the number of priests dropped by some 20 per cent to 32,000, and the number of seminarists receiving ordination fell from over 500 to 111. Most French Catholics now rarely set foot in church except for a christening, a marriage or a funeral. The Church's power to assert itself over moral issues has also diminished, not least because of divisions of opinion within its own ranks.

Laws against contraception, introduced in 1920 to help repair the horrific losses of manpower sustained by France in World War I, were repealed in 1967 despite Catholic opposition, and birth control aids are now freely available. The results are evident in a decline in the birth rate since the mid-1970s; today's average married couple has no more than two children. Abortion too was made legal in 1974, and was soon resorted to widely; by the early 1980s, there were some 22 abortions performed for every 100 children born, a rate ahead of that of any other nation in the Common Market except Denmark and Italy.

Divorce reform, allowing couples to separate by mutual consent if their marriage has broken down, followed in 1975. This measure accelerated a trend toward more frequent divorce than was already evident; now one in every five marriages ends in divorce, and the rate is rising. Statistics show that marital breakdown is most common in urban areas and among couples who marry young. It is most often the wife who sues for an annulment; 68 per cent of women doing so have careers of their own. In the great majority of cases the wife receives custody of the children, and in two out of three cases will also be awarded the family home.

Another prop of the old-style family circle had traditionally been economic need, which prevented the younger generation from leaving home and also

127

6

bonded together networks of relatives in a web of financial interdependence. In rural areas especially, where the extended family was always strongest, the affluence of the postwar years has helped to loosen the ties, as younger members have moved to the cities and suburbs to earn good and dependable salaries there. But if the extended family of grandparents, aunts and cousins has suffered, prosperity has brought a greater well-being to the small, nuclear group, the home unit of parents and children. And in one important respect, that of housing, family life has improved immeasurably during the last two or three decades.

A 1954 census showed that only 10 per cent of all French houses had a bath or a shower and only 27 per cent had indoor lavatories. In the 1960s, the housing shortage was still being described as a national disgrace, and poor housing was frequently blamed for a host of social ills, including crime, suicide and mental illness. Confronted by a growing public outcry, the government at last began to take action and inaugurated a program to build thousands of publicly owned houses and apartments known as HLMs *(habitations à loyer modéré* or low-rent dwellings). At the beginning, these offered little more than a roof over a family's head; rooms were tiny and often there was no bathroom. But standards slowly improved, and between 1954 and 1975 the percentage of homes without a bath or shower dropped from 90 to 23, and those without their own lavatory from 73 to 20. By 1972, some 500,000 units were being built every year, though this rate has now dropped again.

Environmentalists complained bitterly about the barrack-block developments that were rising around every

Among France's 20-million-strong work force, a minority of some 10,000 craftsmen in such skilled trades as plumbing and carpentry belong to an elite fraternity known as *Compagnons du Devoir* ("Companions of Duty"). Tracing their origins back to the Middle Ages, the *compagnons* have evolved rituals reminiscent of freemasonry, among them the initiation ceremony shown above. Apprentices wishing to join are sent on a tour of France, to learn their trade with guild members in different cities; before being accepted, they must produce a large-scale "master work" as evidence of their skill. Membership in the fraternity means a lifelong commitment with an obligation to protect fellow members' interests and maintain high standards of workmanship.

major French city — a phenomenon already common in other European countries — but for the homeless, the HLM program was the most important piece of social legislation since the war. Gradually the housing shortage ceased to be a public scandal. Now improved standards in turn have led to increased expectations, and complaints about HLMs are frequently raised by their residents, the very people who have benefited from the subsidized housing that they provide.

Marcel Rechignac works as a nighttime machine supervisor in a cotton textile factory near Lille in northern France, and lives with his wife and sons in a small, two-story HLM townhouse in the nearby city of Tourcoing, not far from the Belgian border. It is an area of sprawling factories, slag heaps, huge commercial centers and monotonous housing tracts that forms France's fourth largest urban complex.

Reluctantly Marcel admits that his living conditions are superior to those of his parents — they shared a toilet with 10 other houses and a tap with seven families — but he feels that he still has plenty to complain about. Living in a HLM, he says, is "a catastrophe." The rooms are far too cramped to accommodate comfortably a family with three boys aged 20, 17 and 14. HLM regulations decree that two children of the same sex must share a bedroom, regardless of their ages, so the family has only three bedrooms. On the ground floor is a well-equipped kitchen with a washing machine and a freezer, and a living room dominated by a massive television set. Most of their time together indoors is spent sitting around a small linoleum-covered table in this room; apart from fitted wall units (to display a collection of china ornaments and to house bar supplies), a deck chair and a large canary cage, there is little other furniture. The household that assembles here is completed by a well-loved mongrel dog.

Marcel, whose family originally came from the Gard department in Languedoc, is in his midforties, a short, well-built man with a spreading midriff and a double chin that proclaim his fondness for food and drink. His wife Marcelle works in the wool division of a large textile factory, feeding machines with heavy balls of woolen thread; she works from 1 to 9 p.m., so they see little of each other except on weekends. It is inconvenient but necessary: On the night shift Marcel earns 25 per cent more than day-shift workers doing the same job, and the extra money is important to the family budget.

Work for him starts at 9 p.m. and ends at 5 a.m. It is repetitive and boring — "You don't need a diploma from Saint-Cyr to do that kind of job" — and he and his fellow workers resort to numerous short, unofficial cigarette breaks over and above the 20 minutes' rest officially allowed. Marcelle too can find occasional relief from the tiring, standing-up routine by dodging out for a smoke. She earns about three quarters of her husband's salary — slightly more than he would earn on the day shift — and she chose the afternoon shift to have time in the morning to get her sons off to school, do the shopping and the housework, and prepare the lunch boxes for Marcel and herself.

Marcel is a dedicated trade unionist, belonging to the moderate, left-of-center Force Ouvrière union. As such, he serves as a delegate on numerous works committees, including the firm's *comité d'entreprise*. One of his bitterest memories is of losing a previous job for his union activities. As he tells the story, he was offered promotion to the rank of supervisor if he gave up his work with the union. He refused, and eight days later he was fired.

The Rechignacs live on the tightest of budgets and there is little cash left over to cope with sudden crises. The rent for their house, about 15 per cent of Marcel's salary, increases twice a year in line with inflation. They receive a family allowance from the state that almost covers the rent, but this will decrease drastically in a year when Patrick is 18 and considered to be independent.

State benefits are reduced if both father and mother are working, but the Rechignacs calculate that their combined monthly salary is more than they would get from state handouts and Marcel's salary alone. Almost 20 per cent of the earnings go to installment payments on their three-year-old Peugeot and household goods; another 30 per cent goes to housekeeping, which Marcelle budgets with great care, stocking up the freezer by buying in bulk and shopping once a month at a huge discount store. The family enjoys good food. They eat meat every day, often best-quality beef, and this is a luxury for which they are prepared to make sacrifices. As Marcel puts it, "I prefer to spend less on furniture and eat well."

Like the great majority of French workers, the Rechignacs must take their month's vacation in August, and they can usually save enough money to get away. For many years they kept a motor home at Cayeux, between Dieppe and Le Touquet on the Channel coast, but sold it when they decided that paying an annual parking fee for facilities used only once a year was a waste of money. Then for two years

6

they joined the great wave of vacationers traveling south, renting an apartment inland from the Mediterranean resort of St. Raphaël. More recently they have stayed on the Atlantic coast, north of Bordeaux. For Marcel, vacations have become an opportunity to get to know France. As for traveling to a foreign country, the idea has never really been considered.

At home, Marcel's main relaxation is fishing on weekends, and television, almost regardless of the program. Marcelle is less interested in television, and in any case she has little time to herself: Most weekends she is washing, shopping or cleaning the house. When she has a spare moment she likes to visit her sisters at Roubaix nearby. The Rechignacs do not entertain a lot — they like to treat their guests well but cannot afford to do so very often — and they have been to the movies only once in the past eight years. Marcel enjoys reading (usually thrillers), Marcelle does not; neither of them buys or reads a newspaper. Though they did not get married in church, they had their three sons christened, as a matter of custom rather than conviction. Today, Marcel will only visit a church for a christening or a wedding; Marcelle may visit one on other occasions because she likes to listen to church music.

Like all French parents, the Rechignacs are ambitious for their sons, but they are also realistic enough to realize that their paths will not be easy. They long ago accepted that their children were not academically minded, and that the best educational qualifications they could hope for were diplomas preparing them for skilled labor. Marcel, the eldest, dropped out of his joinery course at 17, however, and went to work in a factory for two years, until at

19 he was called up for his compulsory year's military service. Only a few weeks after his return to civilian life, the factory closed down, and he has been out of work ever since. He hopes that the employment agency will help him to take an additional trade training course; if he takes it and is still unable to find work, he will qualify for extra unemployment pay.

Patrick and Bruno are still going to school, hoping to win professional qualifications as roofer and joiner respectively. Their parents would be delighted if they were to achieve them, for they worry that without diplomas their sons will end up as unskilled laborers for the rest of their lives. "My dearest wish," says Marcel, "is that they live a happier life than me and don't have to work nights to earn a living."

The Rechignacs' concern about their children's education is one shared by almost all parents, no matter what their class, for the pressure to do well at school is unrelenting almost from the time that the child first enters the school. If parents so wish, children can start their schooling as early as the age of two, at a state-sponsored *école maternelle*, a nursery school, where they can participate in organized games and other group activities, paint and draw. In their last year at the school, at the age of five, they start learning to read, write and count. These schools are one of the most successful and least criticized elements of their country's state-run education system.

The *école élémentaire*, where children begin their primary education, teaches a basic knowledge of reading, writing and arithmetic; but instead of children progressing together year by year according to age, French children who

have not reached a certain standard are held back, even if they are lagging behind in only parts of the curriculum. Only about half get through elementary school without having to repeat at least one year. Teaching methods vary widely; some schools enforce a strict discipline, while others encourage a relaxed atmosphere in which children address teachers by their first names.

At the age of about 11, the child moves on to a *collège*. In theory, a single system of comprehensive education is offered to every pupil, but in practice the system favors the more privileged, and success is partly determined by the education, status and influence of a child's parents. Serious difficulties usually begin at 13 or 14, during the pupil's third and fourth years, in the grades known collectively as the *cycle d'orientation*. At this stage, an assessment is made of the child's personality, interests and academic ability, to decide which diplomas should be taken; such decisions often settle what a child will do for the rest of his life. Teachers are obliged to take into account the views of both the parents and pupils, and ambitious, upper-class parents are more likely to challenge a teacher's decision successfully than are working-class parents who, with less status and influence, are not as able to ensure a fair deal for their offspring.

From orientation onward, the system pays no more than lip service to the principle of equal opportunity. Children who want to leave school at 16 take an exam before doing so, for a diploma that carries almost no weight at all. Those wanting to learn a trade will have transferred at the age of 13 or 14 to technical training schools, where a two-year course leads to trade qualifications — notably the *certificat d'aptitude*

professionnelle, or CAP — awarded on the basis of classwork and tests.

After *collège,* further academic education is available at a *lycée,* where pupils aged 15 or 16 start to prepare for the dreaded *baccalauréat,* a rigorous and brain-searching examination taken at about 18 which has been described as the national obsession of the French middle class. It is made more daunting by the fact that it is the first public examination the child will have faced in his entire school career. *Le bac* is the passport to higher education — without it no pupil can go on to a university — and the first step to a successful career; failing *le bac* means stigma and the clos-

ing of a spectrum of opportunities.

Pupils preparing for *le bac* can choose from a wide range of subject combinations, of which the most prestigious is "Option C" (maths, science and economics), for that is most likely to open the doors of a *grande école,* the ultimate destination of most ambitious careerists. Of the pupils taking Option C, not more than 5 per cent are likely to come from working-class families.

The ability of the *grandes écoles* to attract the best and the most ambitious students casts a shadow over the prestige of the universities, which by comparison come off second best. Anyone possessing *le bac* may enroll in a univer-

sity. Following reforms in the wake of the student unrest in 1968, the 23 older universities were regrouped into 76 new, smaller and more manageable units. They are semiautonomous bodies, each of which elects its own governing council, on which students are represented. At an academic level, the gulf between staff and students has been narrowed, the ratio of lecturers to students reduced, and greater emphasis has been placed on group work in, for instance, lab classes.

Despite the appeal of these and other reforms, the dropout rate at universities is high. Few state grants are available, and many of the students find the

LOURDES: MONUMENT TO A MIRACLE

The yearning for spiritual aid and the hope of a cure for a multitude of ailments bring some three million visitors annually to the town of Lourdes in southwestern France. Here, in 1858, a 14-year-old peasant girl, Bernadette Soubirous, saw a series of 18 visions of the Virgin Mary in a grotto outside the town. An underground spring she unearthed in the course of one of the visitations was quickly claimed to have miraculous healing powers. The validity of her visions was recognized by the Vatican in 1862, and even before Bernadette's death in 1879, Lourdes had become France's principal place of pilgrimage.

The modern pilgrimage season lasts from April to October, when the sick as well as the healthy gather to bathe in the cold waters of the grotto and to take part in mass displays of popular devotion before the shrine.

Watched by invalids in wheelchairs, stretcher-bound pilgrims form a cross in front of the Lourdes basilica on Ascension Day. Claims of miraculous healing are closely monitored by the Church; of more than 5,000 cases reported between 1878 and 1978, only 64 have been accepted as genuine.

strain of working their way through college too great. Because of the liberal admissions policy, many of the students start their studies without any serious commitment to finishing them or obtaining a degree. In addition, graduate unemployment has been on the rise since the mid-1970s, leading others to question the value of their studies in opening up a career. Realistically, many now accept that a degree, especially in the humanities, opens fewer doors in a competitive job market than a qualification from one of the technical universities set up after 1966 or from one of the specialized colleges that prepare people for work in accountancy, the hotel and catering business, and other trades.

The state school system is complemented by an extensive network of private schools, most of them linked to the Catholic Church. The private schools are subsidized with government money so long as their curriculum includes the subjects taught in the equivalent state schools, but they are free to arrange their timetables to their own convenience and to teach religion. Traditionally it has been the religious emphasis of the schools that has led parents to send their children to them, but in recent years the small classes and strict discipline of many institutions have also had an appeal. Roughly one pupil in six attends a private school, the proportion being highest in the staunchly Catholic areas of Brittany and western France.

Like the Rechignacs, the Tebaldinis worry about education, for they have three children of school age. In other respects, though the two families live in different worlds. The Tebaldinis' home is in the little Burgundian village of Brétigny, which has only about 500 inhabitants and boasts no more than a baker, a grocer, a butcher and a dusty-looking toystore. Extensive shopping facilities are, after all, available some six miles away in and around the city of Dijon, capital of Burgundy. On the outskirts of Brétigny, silhouettes of modern houses contrast sharply with older farms and cottages. The countryside is flat, dominated by large grainfields broken by small woods — and by the network of highways, railroads and canals leading to Dijon.

The Tebaldini family are archetypal members of the upwardly mobile middle class. Claude Tebaldini, aged 36, works with three of his four brothers, running a busy hotel-cum-restaurant on the main Dijon-Langres road. His wife Geneviève, also 36, stays at home to look after the children: Florence, 13, Carole, 10 and five-year-old Fabrice. They live in one of the modern houses on Brétigny's outskirts. Spotlessly clean and neat, it has a well-maintained, large garden. The house is comfortable and well equipped, with modern furniture, two television sets, a video recorder, a new piano, and in the kitchen a dishwasher, an eye-level oven and built-in cabinets. Tiled front steps lead to a large living and dining area, a kitchen, four bedrooms, a bathroom and a shower. In the basement there is a garage, a utility room and a big playroom with a Ping-Pong table. Outside in the driveway are two cars.

As the surname suggests, Claude's family origins are Italian; his grandfather emigrated to France as a boy. Claude's father, now retired, laid the foundations for the Tebaldinis' current prosperity when he bought a quarry and sandpit near Dijon and turned them into a successful business enterprise. He then purchased a run-down bistro and transformed it into the establishment now run by his sons; later he opened a gas station next door. The restaurant has a vast parking lot; in the peak season it caters to as many as 12 tourist buses a day, with fixed-price menus ranging from the cheap to the moderately expensive.

Joining the family business was not without drawbacks for Claude. After training for three years as an apprentice *charcutier,* or pork butcher, he went to work in his father's hotel. There were constant arguments and he often took his talents elsewhere, cooking, working for *charcutiers,* and — during a two-year absence after a particularly bitter disagreement — driving trucks. He met Geneviève when she came to work at the hotel as a waitress. After they were married he settled down, and five years ago, when his father retired, Claude and the three brothers took over the whole business. Since then they have worked hard and prospered, though arguments over the running of the hotel continue and Claude has plans for setting up his own business.

Claude earns substantially more than the two Rechignacs combined — enough to support a comfortable lifestyle of a kind far superior to that of his own youth. An astute property deal bolstered his capital: Ten years ago he bought a house in a new development, sold it seven years later for twice the purchase price, and was able to buy a bigger property next door — their present home — without having to borrow. The price of their new home has also risen steadily; because of its proximity to Dijon, Brétigny has become a very desirable commuter village.

Since neither Claude nor Geneviève got very far at school — she left at 16 with no diplomas, and he acquired only

In a nursery school in Lorient, three children and a teacher busy themselves at a blackboard beneath a banner inscribed with the Breton alphabet.

TEACHING AN ANCIENT TONGUE

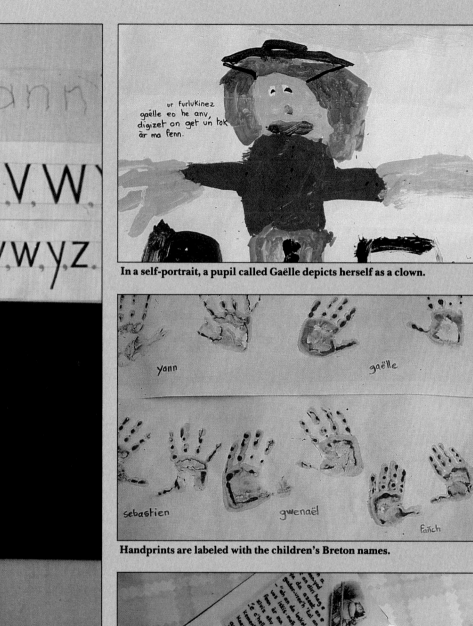

In a self-portrait, a pupil called Gaëlle depicts herself as a clown.

Handprints are labeled with the children's Breton names.

A child reads a story whose French text is masked by a Breton translation.

France has not always spoken one language. Occitan, still heard in the south, was once as widely used as French; and Brittany in the northwest — peopled by Britons fleeing Angle and Saxon invaders in the Fifth and Sixth centuries — was for hundreds of years an independent land with its own Celtic tongue, more closely related to Welsh and Cornish than to Latin-derived French. By the time Brittany was incorporated into France in 1532, distinctive identity and culture had taken deep root.

For the next 250 years, the region resisted centralization, but in the 19th Century the government in Paris tried to assimilate its people. The Breton language was forbidden, and children were punished if they spoke it at school. Breton-speakers became a minority in their own land; today only about a quarter of Brittany's 2.5 million people speak the language.

Since the 1960s, however, the state has reversed its policy under pressure from Breton nationalists, and the local culture is now tolerated and even encouraged. The new mood bore fruit in 1977 when pioneers of a Breton-language revival campaign opened a nursery school in which toddlers are taught in their own tongue. In 1978, seven such schools were founded; by 1983 there were 25, with 40 teachers and 300 children. Each gives two- to six-year-olds basic grounding in Breton before they attend state primary schools where only French is spoken.

The future of the schools, funded by voluntary contribution, is far from assured, however, and prospects for the language are still in doubt. Opportunities for speaking it are limited, and radio and TV companies broadcast few Breton-language programs. Despite the new government policy, its fate rests with the Bretons; if the language is to survive, it will only do so by popular demand and — literally — by word of mouth.

6

a minor technical qualification—they are especially anxious for their children to shine academically. Florence is in fact doing well at a *collège* in Dijon, having regularly been at the top of her class in the *école élémentaire*. She is already expressing an interest in studying to become a pediatrician, an ambition her parents support. The two younger children are at the local *école élémentaire,* Carole in her last year and Fabrice in his first. Fabrice is nearly a year ahead; at the age of five, he would normally still be at an *école maternelle,* but the town has none and he is taking the first-year primary school subjects, the curriculum of the so-called *cycle préparatoire.*

In the home Geneviève bears the brunt of the responsibility for bringing up the children. She helps them with their homework and encourages them to persevere at whatever they may be doing: Florence, for instance, enjoys gymnastics and ballet. Claude thinks that Geneviève is a lot stricter than he would be. When Florence was a troublesome, self-willed toddler, a pediatrician recommended a *martinet*—a leather thong for chastisement—to bring her to heel. Geneviève bought one and has not hesitated to use it, or at least to threaten to use it, on all three children. She says that it is a very effective deterrent to bad behavior.

Home and family fully occupy Geneviève. She admits to no interest in any other career, but is always prepared to help her husband in his work, and until Florence was born she continued as a waitress at the hotel. She and Claude agree that looking after a house, a large garden and three school-age children is a full-time occupation for her.

Claude does not help around the house much, nor is he expected to, although occasionally he will prepare a meal. At the hotel he normally supervises the shopping and the cooking, while his brothers take care of the administration. He works one week from 6:30 a.m. to 3 p.m. and the next from 2:30 p.m. to midnight, an arrangement that suits him as it gives him plenty of leisure time. He enjoys bicycling, anything up to 50 miles a day, and a new French passion—jogging.

Among the rewards of financial success have been some memorable vacations. Claude cannot leave the hotel during the tourist season—just at the time of the children's summer vacation—but in the autumn he and Geneviève have gone away for the past three years, to Kenya, the Seychelles and Morocco, and Geneviève's mother has taken care of the children. In the summer, Geneviève and the children go away for a month to the beach, where they stay in a rented apartment or a cottage. And earlier this year the whole family managed a week's cross-country skiing in Switzerland.

The Tebaldinis are not particularly interested in politics, national or local, and with the exception of the local daily paper and a television program guide, they rarely buy newspapers or magazines. Claude clings tenaciously to free-market economic principles; if you work hard, you make money, your business grows and you create jobs. He views socialism with distinctly jaundiced eyes. Social changes like increased sexual freedom and divorce worry neither of them too much, and they welcome the fact that their children feel free to ask questions about sex that they themselves would never have dared to ask when young. Although both of them were confirmed and they had a church wedding, they come from essentially nonreligious families, nor does religion have any importance in their own lives. They do not intend to force their children to be confirmed.

The kind of old-fashioned discipline represented by the *martinet* occasionally wielded by Geneviève Tebaldini has recently been on the wane in France. The tendency of the past two decades has been toward a more open society in which social contact between parents and children, as between the sexes, is more relaxed. The inspiration for such new liberalism came largely from the student revolt of 1968. Politically the uprising failed to achieve its objectives, and indeed few of its leaders seemed clear about what those objectives were; but the social ideas expressed then with explosive force have influenced society from that time, encouraging freedom and debate at the expense of discipline and hierarchy.

The changes have been particularly marked in relations between the sexes. One evident symbol of sexual liberation has been the widespread acceptance of couples living together before marriage; four out of 10 couples arriving at the altar have been cohabiting before the ceremony, on the average for some two years. Not that marriage as an institution is under threat, or promiscuity rampant. In some ways, the idea of cohabiting has simply replaced the tradition of a formal engagement.

Another tendency that has affected family life in the past few decades has been the rise of feminism. The women's liberation movement took longer to gather momentum in France than in the United States or Britain, largely because of an ambivalence in the attitude of French women, who tend to prize femininity above emancipation. When it won widespread support, through the influence of the media and women's magazines, it did so by deliberately spurning the more aggressive and masculine aspects of the movement. French women have no vestiges of an inferiority complex to cloud their relations with men, for they have always regarded themselves as equal but different, and *le droit à la différence* — the right to be different — became one of the movement's slogans. French women now ex-pect equal pay and opportunities as a right — but they still want to be courted and flattered and to benefit from the innumerable little gallantries with which French men have traditionally paid them homage.

At French universities, the proportion of female students is now 46 per cent, and in most arts courses women now form a solid majority. Some 10 per cent of students at the École Polytech-nique, once a male bastion, are now women. The increased prosperity of the postwar years has also increased choice of employment for women of all classes. Working-class wives, who have traditionally had to work to help support their families, now have the possibility of staying at home. Conversely, women of the middle and upper classes are now more likely to have jobs, and it is becoming common for a wife's career

At a book fair held just after the start of the school year, a student at a *lycée* in the Norman city of Caen holds up books he wishes to sell. The atmosphere for these academically able 15-to 18-year-olds is relaxed — a legacy of the changes in educational attitudes after the troubles of May 1968.

6

to demand as much time and effort, and to be rewarded with as high a salary, as her husband's. The strains within many marriages today no longer resemble those described by Gustave Flaubert in his novel *Madame Bovary* — the bored, frustrated housewife with too little to occupy her; instead, the problems are likely to be those of an ambitious working mother coping with the stress of having too many demands made on her time.

Françoise Lepercq is well aware of the problems that combining work and a family can cause: She has many friends whose marriages have broken up for that reason. Yet she herself has found fulfillment through her career, which she only started 10 years after her marriage. The very model of the urban professional woman, she is lively, talkative and intelligent, with an effortless dress sense and the looks that could let her pass as her daughter's elder sister. Her husband, Luc, is a tall, quiet man in his midforties. Once a naval officer specializing in deep-water diving research, he subsequently held executive positions with three companies before taking up his present job as projects manager with an oil company. They have two sons, Thierry, 21, and Nicolas, 17, and two daughters, Sandra, 18, and Juliette, 11.

The Lepercqs own a five-bedroom apartment, furnished comfortably, on the top two floors of a large house in Suresnes, a residential suburb on the western fringe of Paris. They have lived there for six years. Like many well-connected French couples, they also have access to numerous country residences that are owned by members of their families. These include a huge, fortified farmhouse, complete with tur-

At a municipal day-care nursery in central Paris, a father sets his baby in a crib *(top)* and a mother leaves her son with the supervisor *(above)*. France is relatively well provided with child-care centers, most funded by state or local authorities; of 200 in Paris, only 25 are privately owned.

rets, not far from Chambéry in Savoy, which has been in Luc's family for generations; he now owns it with a brother and sister. On Françoise's side there is a large old house near Avignon, a villa on the Côte d'Azur, and an apartment in the Alps they use for skiing vacations.

Thierry, the elder son, is in his last year at the École des Hautes Études Commerciales (HEC), the leading *grande école* in the field of business studies. As such, its graduates are virtually swamped with job offers; but Thierry plans after graduation to spend a year in America at a university in North Carolina, lecturing part time and taking another course of studies. After that he will return to France to complete his military service, and only then make a final career decision. Like most well-educated young Frenchmen, he will opt to do his service working abroad for one and a half to two years in an underdeveloped country, rather than endure the alternative of one year's conventional military training. Thierry is lucky — as his mother admits — that he is under no financial pressure to start work. As for the other children, Sandra and Nicolas are taking their *baccalauréat* this summer, while Juliette, the youngest, is at the local *collège* in Suresnes.

Françoise left the university before she completed her studies in order to marry Luc; she spent the first 10 years of married life, in her words, "having babies and moving," as Luc's naval career led the family to different posts. It was when Thierry was 10 that she first felt the need for a job. The family was then living in Toulon. She began writing articles on sociocultural subjects for a monthly magazine. When the family moved to Paris six years ago, she set about building a proper career as a journalist. First she worked in the press departments of two ministries, then as an intern at the influential daily newspaper *Le Monde*, and after that she took a government-subsidized journalism course. For the past two years, however, she has had a fulfilling job outside journalism; she markets and runs courses for business employees on such themes as adolescence, retirement and married life, the aim being to close the gap between family and professional life. As Françoise frequently has to be away from home in her work, often for a week at a time, the family has had to reorganize itself to cope with household duties. Luc takes on the responsibility for the children when she is away.

The Lepercqs are well traveled. The three eldest children have spent vacations, arranged by international organizations, in America and England; and Thierry has been on a trip to India arranged by the HEC during which he and his fellow students helped with a small village construction project. In addition, Luc and Françoise try to spend some time with the children every year on an activity vacation — sailing, skiing, walking or climbing. Of their own brothers and sisters — Luc has no less than 12, Françoise four — the Lepercq parents see relatively little in the course of the year.

At home, reading is a leisure activity enjoyed by all the family. They get *Le Monde* every day, *Libération* — an independent newspaper politically to the left — occasionally, and a number of magazines, including the UNESCO review which is read by all of them. Françoise in particular is an avid reader, mainly of informative nonfiction, whether it be history or child psychology books, and she is quite prepared to tackle esoteric scientific works. It is a passion she has been happy to communicate to her children.

Luc and Françoise are believers, though neither goes regularly to mass or to confession. For them religion means accepting a spiritual dimension to their lives and living according to Christian principles. Politically, Luc has wavered between right and left over the years, while Françoise has always been leftist — a reaction, she says, against her right-wing father, an École Polytechnique graduate who was a director of the state electricity company. She dreams of a world in which everyone has equal opportunities and the ability to fulfill his or her potential — but she is sometimes very pessimistic about it ever coming to pass.

Françoise feels that they are a close and happy family, with only small conflicts. She would also admit that they are fortunate to belong to a privileged milieu that has made their path easier than that of most French people. Yet the easygoing relationships the Lepercqs share are in many ways symptomatic of the social changes that have filtered slowly through the entire social structure in the past 20 years. Gone, for the most part, are the old authoritarian homes in which the father ruled with an iron hand. But gone too are the more extreme demands of the days of 1968, when the very survival of the family was called into question, and communes and sexual freedom were the order of the day. Instead, a compromise solution has slowly evolved, by which the most resented features of the old nuclear unit — the lack of dialogue, the imposition of one person's will — have been largely jettisoned, but the institution itself has been saved in a more open and freer form. The family is dead; long live the family! □

AN APPETITE FOR IDEAS

Tourists and students mingle in a café on Paris' Boulevard St. Michel, the main thoroughfare of the capital's university district. Such Left Bank watering-holes have traditionally been places for exchanging ideas — but also for starting flirtations and studying fashions.

At least since the Renaissance, the inhabitants of France have tended to regard their country as the true center of civilization, the pacesetter in the art of living. In the 17th and 18th Centuries, French culture did indeed attain a position of rare preeminence in the world. The military might and the prestige of King Louis XIV carried the nation's manners and styles across the continent of Europe, and the reflected glory of the Sun King set a fashion for extravagant and grandiose display among the upper classes of many lands. For a century or more, the rulers of dozens of central European principalities and duchies imported French architects and designers to build reduced-scale copies of the Palace of Versailles in their capitals, and French chamberlains and stewards supervised the ceremonies that took place within them.

Even more extraordinary was the triumph of the French language. The influence of writers and thinkers of the 18th Century Enlightenment — among them Voltaire and Rousseau, Montesquieu and Diderot — traversed national frontiers. With France triumphant in matters both of taste and of intellect, wealthy families from Vienna to St. Petersburg felt the need to hire French tutors for their children. Major foreign writers, including the German philosopher Baron Gottfried von Leibnitz and the English historian Edward Gibbon, wrote fluently in French as a second language; the great Goethe even

toyed briefly with the idea of using it instead of German as his principal means of expression.

French was the daily tongue of the courts of Frederick the Great of Prussia, of the Holy Roman Emperor Joseph II and of Catherine the Great, Empress of Russia. In the early 19th Century Marshal Bernadotte, the Napoleonic general chosen by the Swedes to be their king, ruled for more than a quarter of a century without speaking a word of Swedish. All official business was conducted in French.

In the wake of its adoption as the language of Europe's courts came the ascendancy of French as the language of diplomacy. The first international accords to be drafted exclusively in it were the treaties of Utrecht and Rastatt, which brought to an end the War of the Spanish Succession in 1714. By the early 19th Century, it was accepted as the obligatory language of diplomatic correspondence across Europe, used even for private communications between rulers. Sometimes its applications were bizarre; in 1882, the documents cementing the Triple Alliance of Germany, Austro-Hungary and Italy against France were drawn up in French, and in 1905 it was the language used to bring to an end the Russo-Japanese War, fought in the Pacific halfway across the world from France. The tradition only began to weaken in 1919, when the Treaty of Versailles, concluding World War I, was drafted

141

in twin versions, one in French and the other in English.

By that time French had ceased to be a lingua franca for the ruling classes of Europe, and French literature was no longer without rival as a continental pacesetter. Its hegemony had first been challenged in the early 19th Century by the coming of the Romantic movement, whose leaders turned to German and English models for inspiration. Nonetheless, the ensuing century had been a golden age of French writing, and its masters — Stendhal, Balzac, Hugo, Flaubert, Maupassant, Zola — continued to exert powerful influences. The early 20th Century brought new talents, with the fiction of Marcel Proust, Louis-Ferdinand Céline and André Gide and the poetry of Paul Claudel and Paul Valéry leading the way.

So France's eclipse as a literary Great Power was only relative. Besides generating an unceasing flow of talent, the nation continued to accord high prestige to ideas and the people who gave voice to them. The nation's educational system has traditionally been geared to the humanities, and even today, when the sciences are beginning to gain an increasing share of the curriculum, it is obligatory for all secondary-school students in their final year to take a course in philosophy. The ability to express oneself well is highly prized, and authors, who naturally possess that talent to the fullest degree, are treated with a respect that foreign writers look upon with envy.

Symptomatic of the high regard felt for writers and writing is the fact that every president of the Fifth Republic has had literary aspirations. General de Gaulle was the author of classic memoirs and speeches and a brilliant exponent of the French language, able to bring together nobility and earthiness in a singly pithy and memorable phrase. His successor, Georges Pompidou, was a former literature teacher who published a noted anthology of French poetry. Valéry Giscard d'Estaing wrote a book of political theory while in office and once sadly confessed that his greatest ambition had been to be a writer. Before becoming president, François Mitterrand authored a dozen or so works on political and economic themes, and described himself as an avid reader who often finished several volumes in a week.

The high standing traditionally accorded to authors can confer practical benefits on men of letters. As long ago as the 15th Century, the vagabond poet François Villon, condemned to death for robbery and manslaughter, was released on the orders of Charles VII who considered Villon's poetic talent too valuable to waste on the gallows. As recently as 1970, Régis Debray, the Marxist intellectual and comrade of Che Guevara, was freed from a Bolivian jail largely as a result of pleas for clemency made on his behalf by the government of Georges Pompidou. Although the petitioners were his political opponents, they felt that Debray was nonetheless entitled to the privilege due to his status as a writer.

No institution more succinctly encapsulates the continuing high status of literature in French society than the Académie Française, an august and unique body that is also the most obvious legacy of the 17th Century golden age to the present day. The Academy was established in 1635 by Cardinal Richelieu, then chief minister and the nation's true ruler during the reign of Louis XIII. The cardinal's spies had reported to him that a group of writers were holding regular meetings for the purpose of discussing literary and linguistic topics. Like most autocrats, Richelieu was suspicious of any gatherings that he could not control himself. But whereas a lesser man would have banned the meetings, Richelieu virtually conscripted the participants into the royal service by making them the core of his Academy, charged with the maintenance of good taste in French language and style.

The Academy outlived the monarchy and has survived comfortably to the days of the Fifth Republic. In recent times it has had little influence and has often been derided by its opponents as an Establishment mouthpiece or a complacent club of pedants. But it has never lacked for would-be members. And like all good survivors, it has shown the ability to embrace forces potentially hostile to it. So the author and film maker Jean Cocteau, figurehead of the avant-garde, was elected to the Academy in 1955; and more recently the growing feminist movement was recognized by the election of the historical novelist Marguerite Yourcenear, the first woman member.

The most recent literary flowering in France came with the conclusion of World War II, when a new generation of politically committed writers came to the fore under the inspiration of the two masters of the mid-20th Century, Albert Camus and Jean-Paul Sartre. In the way of Left Bank intellectuals, the two writers were to part company over politics despite a shared background in the wartime Resistance to Nazi occupation; the point of contention was Sartre's espousal of Soviet-style Communism. Both men continued to produce works that mingled philosophy,

A GREAT TRADITION IN THE ARTS

France's record of achievement in the arts is almost unparalleled in its extent and its duration. The chart below lists a selection of the nation's outstanding creators in the fields of literature, music and the fine arts from the Middle Ages to the present century.

	LITERATURE	MUSIC	FINE ARTS
1400	François Villon 1431-?		Jean Fouquet c.1415-c.1480
1500	François Rabelais ?1497-1553 Pierre de Ronsard 1524-1585 Michel de Montaigne 1533-1592		François Clouet c.1516-c.1572
1600	René Descartes 1596-1650 Molière 1622-1673 (Jean-Baptiste Poquelin) Blaise Pascal 1623-1662 Jean Racine 1639-1699	Jean-Baptiste Lully 1632-1687	Georges de la Tour 1593-1652 Nicolas Poussin 1594-1665 Claude Lorrain 1600-1682
1700	Charles de Montesquieu 1689-1755 Voltaire 1694-1778 (François-Marie Arouet) Jean-Jacques Rousseau 1712-1778 Denis Diderot 1713-1784	François Couperin 1668-1733 Jean-Philippe Rameau 1683-1764	Antoine Watteau 1684-1721 Jean-Baptiste Chardin 1699-1779 François Boucher 1703-1770 Jean-Honoré Fragonard 1732-1806

1800	Stendhal 1783-1842
	  (Henri Beyle)
	Honoré Balzac 1799-1850
	Victor Hugo 1802-1885
	
	Gustave Flaubert 1821-1880
	Charles Baudelaire 1821-1867
	
	Émile Zola 1840-1902
	Stéphane Mallarmé 1842-1898
	Paul Verlaine 1844-1896
	Guy de Maupassant 1850-1893
	Arthur Rimbaud 1854-1891
		Hector Berlioz 1803-1869
		
		Camille Saint-Saëns 1835-1921
		Georges Bizet 1838-1875
		
		Emmanuel Chabrier 1841-1894
		Gabriel Fauré 1845-1924
			Jacques-Louis David 1748-1825
			Jean-Auguste-Dominique Ingres
			  1780-1867
			Théodore Géricault 1791-1824
			Camille Corot 1796-1875
			Eugène Delacroix 1798-1863
			Honoré Daumier 1808-1879
			Gustave Courbet 1819-1877
			Camille Pissarro 1830-1903
			Édouard Manet 1832-1883
			Edgar Degas 1834-1917
			Paul Cézanne 1839-1906
			Claude Monet 1840-1926
			Auguste Rodin 1840-1917
			Pierre-Auguste Renoir 1841-1919
			Henri Rousseau 1844-1910
			Paul Gauguin 1848-1903
			Georges Seurat 1859-1891
			Henri de Toulouse-Lautrec 1864-1901

1900	Paul Claudel 1868-1955 André Gide 1869-1951 Paul Valéry 1871-1945 Marcel Proust 1871-1922 Colette 1873-1954 Guillaume Apollinaire 1880-1918 Jean Giraudoux 1882-1944 François Mauriac 1885-1970 Jean Cocteau 1889-1963 Louis-Ferdinand Céline 1894-1961 André Malraux 1901-1976 Jean-Paul Sartre 1905-1980 Albert Camus 1913-1960	Claude Debussy 1862-1918 Erik Satie 1866-1925 Maurice Ravel 1875-1937 Darius Milhaud 1892-1974 Arthur Honegger 1892-1955 Francis Poulenc 1899-1963	Henri Matisse 1869-1954 Pierre Bonnard 1867-1947 Georges Rouault 1871-1958 Maurice de Vlaminck 1876-1958 Raoul Dufy 1877-1953 André Derain 1880-1954 Fernand Léger 1881-1955 Georges Braque 1882-1963 Maurice Utrillo 1883-1955 Marcel Duchamp 1887-1968 Jean Arp 1887-1966 Nicolas de Staël 1914-1955

7

drama and fiction, until fate intervened cruelly in 1960 when, three years after receiving the Nobel Prize for literature, Camus was killed in a car crash at the tragically early age of 46. Thus was removed from the literary scene a figure whose influence might well have proved critical in the troubled decades of the 1960s and 1970s.

Sartre had established his philosophical reputation during the Occupation years as the author of *Being and Nothingness,* a treatise that was to become one of the key texts of existentialism. The movement itself did not originate with him or even in France: Its history can be traced back at least as far as the 19th Century Danish Christian thinker Søren Kierkegaard. Such thinking struck a deep chord in French hearts, however, in the gray, grim years of the Occupation and the reconstruction that followed. As expressed by Sartre, existentialism became a philosophy dealing directly with the ineluctable moral problems confronting mankind in a universe assumed to be atheistic and absurd; condemned to freedom, mankind must choose responsibility for his actions, however gratuitous, without divine assistance.

In the late 1940s and 1950s, existentialism became first a cult and then a fashion. The Left Bank was à la mode and the image of its café-philosophers seized the imagination of a whole generation of comfortably disaffected youth. In bars and smoky jazz cellars in Paris itself and as far away as London's Soho and New York's Greenwich Village, eager converts gathered to proclaim themselves existentialists. Sartre himself was so badgered by onlookers that he fled from the cafés he used to haunt; the philosopher had become a tourist attraction.

In the manner of intellectual fashions, existentialism burned itself out in the 1960s, although not before its particular brand of romantic pessimism had left an indelible mark on the consciousness of the West. Sartre himself had qualified his support for Russian Communism after the Hungarian uprising of 1956 was suppressed by Soviet troops, and subsequently distanced

himself from it still further to adopt the position of an independent critic of the left. He retained a unique charisma until his death in 1980.

For a time it looked as though existentialism would have no successor as a dominant intellectual mode, but then a number of parallel developments came together to spawn a system of thought that seemed more in keeping with the

Strollers on the Left Bank around the turn of the century enjoy one of Paris' abiding pleasures — browsing among the bookstalls that line the Seine. Dating back to the mid-19th Century, stall-owners are licensed for business by the municipal council.

technologies of postwar France: structuralism. Like existentialism, structuralism is an international movement that has taken particularly firm root in France. In its least specialized and probably most useful form, it is not so much a philosophy as a method of thinking that applies itself to almost every art and most sciences. It consists of looking at facts and events not in isolation but as part of a whole, a structure; and in recognizing that it is the structure that is important, and not its component parts, which have no meaningful existence on their own.

Thus simply expressed, structuralism appears little more than an enunciation of the obvious. In practice, it is anything but straightforward. It began in linguistics, when American researchers developed an analysis of language that insisted that every quirk of grammar or vocabulary was rooted in a kind of "deep structure" that itself helped to define and explain the totality of human culture. From there it spread to France and to other disciplines, notably anthropology, where Claude Lévi-Strauss used its methods to examine the concealed structure underlying social life. Though Lévi-Strauss' own works were illuminated by the spark of an original and lively mind, that of other structuralists was less inspiring. In the hands of its apologists, the structuralist movement generated an immense and specialized vocabulary, threatening to include all known phenomena in vaster and vaster structures until at last every possible fact or observation had jelled into pure thought.

In the course of its development, structuralism has provided powerful insights into subjects as far apart as biology and literary criticism. However, the theory's very real value only partly ac-

On a cold April day in 1980, a crowd of 30,000 mourners follows the funeral cortège of philosopher Jean-Paul Sartre to Paris' Montparnasse cemetery. The leading exponent of Existentialism, he used novels and plays to popularize his ideas for a worldwide audience.

counts for the enthusiasm with which it has been adopted by France's intellectuals and the delight with which it has been received by their peers abroad.

Arguably as important has been the effect of structuralism in redefining intellectuals as a permanent cultural elite. In the 1950s and 1960s, the intellectual community felt increasingly outside the mainstream of national development, as the nation's leadership concentrated on the engineers and administrators largely responsible for France's fast-expanding economy. Structuralism gave it a rallying-point. The theory's proliferating jargon, gloriously complex and increasingly incomprehensible to outsiders, provided it with something akin to a language of its own. The fact that the theory claims to be able to explain all human experience as a totality places its exponents in a commanding position over mere technocrats.

As a dominant theory, structuralism seems likely to continue for some time. In its way, it is at least as fashionable as existentialism ever was, although it is a fashion confined to high intellectual circles. In one sense, it could be said to be the intellectual equivalent of the inward-turning mood in which so much of France seeks fulfillment today.

On a less exalted intellectual plane, philosophy made the headlines in the late 1970s with the emergence of a group of young writers, who were quickly christened, with a typical Parisian enthusiasm for novelty, the *nouveaux philosophes*. What was new about this group, led by André Glucksmann and Bernard-Henri Lévy, was not so much their ideas as their politics, which, influenced by the Russian writer Alexander Solzhenitsyn's revelations about the Gulags of the Soviet Union, moved away from the Marxist left. This change in itself was sufficient to cause a stir: Since the end of World War II, the terms "intellectual" and "man of the left" had often seemed synonymous.

The new philosophers themselves have not yet made a strong impact on French intellectual life, and there are plenty of voices raised among their political opponents to claim that their significance has been exaggerated by a largely right-wing press. But the advent of the *nouveaux philosophes* is symptomatic of a newly questioning spirit on social matters; the common political front of the Parisian intelligentsia has to some small extent been breached.

In the literary world no great names have arisen to take the place of Sartre and Camus, though many fine books are still being written. The fashion for the "new novel" — the school of literature, pioneered by such writers as Alain Robbe-Grillet and Michel Butor, which sought to remove the emotional element from literary description and replace it with a scientifically exact approach to the outside world — peaked in the 1960s, and has since been in decline. The acclaimed novels of the 1970s were a diverse bunch, reflecting a more intimate and personal mood. They included Michel Tournier's Gothic fantasy, *Le Roi des Aulnes (The Erl King)*; Jean Carrière's bleak study of the harsh life of peasants in the Cévennes, *L'Épervier de Maheux (The Maheux Sparrow-Hawk)*; and among more commercially successful titles, Robert Sabatier's delicate study of a middle-class childhood between the wars, *Les Allumettes Suédoises (The Swedish Matches)*, and Patrick Modiano's affectionate existentialist parody of 1940s detective thrillers, *Rue des Boutiques Obscures (Missing Persons)*.

Despite fears that the growth of the electronic media would kill off the reading habit, the audience for books in France is actually increasing. A statistical survey carried out by the Ministry of Culture in the early 1980s indicated that 74 per cent of those questioned had read at least one book in the preceding 12 months, as against slightly less than 70 per cent in a similar survey conducted in 1973. The vast majority of books sold, however, are bought by a minority of the population, estimated at around 20 per cent, who claim to read a book every two weeks. There is no extensive public library system — only one person in five has a library card — and the number of titles published each year is far lower than in either Britain or West Germany. Apart from the popular spy thrillers, detective stories and family sagas that make up much of the French bestseller lists, successful titles tend to depend on a favorable reception from the charmed circle of Parisian literary critics. A book that is not discussed in the right places will not sell, and the right places are few.

The circle extends its influence into the world of literary prizes, essential yardsticks of success in a competitive, meritocratic society that values culture. Astonishing though it may seem, there are some 1,500 such prizes available, awarded by national and provincial academies and a diversity of juries. At the top end of the spectrum are the Prix Goncourt (created in 1903 to reward a prose work published during the year), the Fémina (chosen by an all-woman jury), the Médicis (intended to reward novelty of style or approach), the Interallié (generally awarded to a novel by a journalist) and the Renaudot (conceived as a supplement and corrective to the Goncourt); at the lower end are prizes for works by railway men, post office employees and other occupational groups. Most of them are awarded in the late autumn, with an eye to boosting Christmas sales. In this firmament the Goncourt is still the most brilliant star. Besides conferring prestige, it can boost the sales of a winning title by 100,000 copies or more. Although intended to reward young writers, it has often gone to those with an established reputation, including a sexagenarian, Lucien Bodard, in 1981.

If the literary intelligentsia have seen their influence decline in the postwar years, it is in part because the power of the written word has been challenged and to some extent supplanted by the rise of the broadcasting media. Television is by now easily the most important of these, though it got off to a slow start in France. Until 1964, the nation had only one channel; a third was not added until 1973. The 1960s were the period when television viewing became a regular part of French life; the number of sets in use rose from one million to 10 million in the course of the decade. The figures continued to rise, though more slowly, through the following decade, until by 1980 nearly 16 million sets were in use.

Creatively, until recently, the whole French broadcasting system was held down firmly under the hand of state control. The French government recognized the immense power of the medium long before the intellectuals: If television was to be the plaything of anyone, it would be the state's.

The Office de la Radio et de la Télévision Française (ORTF) was formed after World War II as a monopoly broadcasting organization under the direct control of the Ministry of Information. The effect was twofold. First, in news and current affairs, French television was notoriously the voice of the government. Secondly, since political reliability rather than creative skill was the criterion for promotion within the organization, programs of every sort tended to be dull, even amateurish; the ORTF grew as government departments will, into a swollen bureaucracy in which administrators outnumbered producers by almost 50 to one.

In some respects, government intentions, at least, were good. There was no television advertising; imported soap operas were sternly discouraged; and particularly during the de Gaulle years, when the novelist André Malraux was Minister of Culture, many of the programs were devoted to the arts. But viewers found that the combination of servility and dullness was unattractive — so much so that by 1965 the French people owned only half as many television sets as their British counterparts and a third as many as the Americans.

The situation worsened, if anything, after the ORTF staff rebelled during the social upheavals of the 1960s and were subsequently whipped back into line by wholesale firings and demotions. To help counterbalance the growing cost of the service to the nation, some advertising was permitted after 1968, but more sweeping changes had to wait until 1974, when Giscard

A cartoon by the humorist Sempé pokes gentle fun at the elevated intellectual level of some French television shows. The caption reads: "Now I'd like to put to you the question that all our viewers must be asking themselves: How does your oneiric conception, with its Kafkaesque implications, coexist with the sublogical vision you have of intrinsic being?"

— Maintenant, je voudrais vous poser la question que doivent se poser tous nos téléspectateurs : Comment votre concept onirique à tendance kafkaïenne coexiste-t-il avec la vision sublogique que vous faites de l'existence intrinsèque ?

d'Estaing was elected president.

Giscard abolished the ORTF and replaced it with seven smaller organizations, including one for each of the three television channels and a production company to supply them with new programs. Instead of producing a healthy spirit of competition as hoped, however, the new structure merely encouraged an unseemly scramble for the audience ratings that by 1980 saw France importing at least 50 per cent of its televised material, most of it in the form of American soap operas. News and current affairs programs continued to shy away from carrying any material that might be an embarrassment to the government, and the entire broadcasting network still suffered from a problem that had debilitated the ORTF: an inability to attract first-class talents from the movie industry, because people could work there with less interference and make more money.

The failings of the Giscard reforms led to another reorganization when the socialist President Mitterrand came to power. A new High Authority was created with the express intention of guaranteeing the independence of radio and television. Changes were also made in the method of financing the different channels. Under Giscard, money had been allocated more or less in proportion to a channel's popularity; in the future the sums of money were to be decided according to project costs, thus diminishing the need for ratings wars. The reforms were generally accepted by most shades of political opinion in France, but only time can tell whether they will prove sufficient to break the old bad habits.

After the expansion of the Giscard years, television viewing has settled into a regular pattern. More than nine in 10 French households now possess a television set, and the average Frenchman spends more than two hours a day in front of it. A typical day's programming includes the same balance of news, sports, films and soaps to be found in most Western countries. In recent years, political debates have also become a feature of the small screen, and these face-to-face confrontations between leading politicians, which attract large audiences, have a marked influence on public opinion.

The situation with regard to radio is more complicated. The state finances three stations: France-Culture, France-Musique — both cultural in orientation and drawing relatively small audiences — and France-Inter, a national channel broadcasting music, news and discussion 24 hours a day. These organizations are supplemented by regional broadcasts and by so-called peripheral stations, largely French owned but broadcasting into France from transmitters outside French territory, so as to circumvent the state monopoly. The most popular of these networks are Europe 1, in the Saar region of West Germany, Radio-Télé-Luxembourg, the national station of the grand Duchy, and the smaller Radio Monte Carlo.

From a street stand, a provincial news agent offers a bewildering variety of periodicals, while a lone Parisian (right) reads a newspaper in a city park. The circulation of Paris-based dailies has sunk to less than half its prewar level, but magazine sales have been rising steadily.

The government winks at this situation, though not without some misgivings; it has taken steps to ensure that state interests have a prominent voice among the shareholders of each station.

The mid-1970s saw a threat to the state monopoly from a different quarter when a rash of pirate radio stations, encouraged by the loosening of governmental reins under Giscard, began broadcasting illegally from tiny transmitters around the country. Some stations were frankly commercial, others political, many amateurish. To bring the situation under control, President Mitterrand, who had given his support to one such station under socialist control in 1979 and had been fined for doing so, made a selective authorization of the transmitters; but the low broadcasting wattage allowed to them, and a ban on accepting advertising revenue, has effectively limited their influence.

It is possible to exaggerate the power of the electronic media to affect public opinion in a land where family ties and word of mouth still carry much political weight. After all, the government's broadcasting patronage did not succeed in preventing a landslide vote for the opposition in the 1981 presidential elections. Yet there are special features of the print media in France that tend to increase the importance of television and radio broadcasts.

To begin with, France no longer has a truly national press; the power of the Parisian dailies has sadly diminished. In the days before World War II, the capital supported 30 newspapers; now barely a dozen survive. The distribution network that carried the metropolitan papers out to the provinces was disrupted during the Occupation years, during which the provincial press substantially increased its share of total readership. The trend continued

7

after the war, and since 1960 the Paris papers have lost another million readers between them.

The chief success story of the postwar years in Parisian journalism has been *Le Monde,* an influential and intellectually elevated daily that boasts an average circulation of about half a million copies. *Le Monde,* which surprisingly appears not in the morning but in the early afternoon, was launched as a successor to a prewar newspaper called *Le Temps.* Its first director, Hubert Beuve-Méry, was a radical Catholic who had resigned from *Le Temps* at the time of the Munich agreements to protest against the paper's support for a policy of appeasing Hitler. Today, the editorial staff holds a controlling interest in the newspaper and elect their own editor-in-chief.

Le Monde is written for a small minority of decision makers, a minority to which its hundreds of thousands of other readers outside their ranks can vicariously belong. Its style is deliberately austere — the reader is rarely helped by such conveniences as typographical variety or photographs — and that austerity also extends to the way in which its articles are written. The punch line of a story may not be discovered in the lead but in a dropped phrase, a piece of buried treasure, which the attentive reader will dig up deep in the foothills of exposition and comment, and which will tell him, in a nutshell, just how the political kaleidoscope has shifted in the last 24 hours.

Le Monde is exceptional among the Paris dailies for its rising number of readers. In general the provincial press is in a much healthier state. The bestselling newspaper in France, *Ouest-France* with a circulation of some 700,000, is based in Brittany. Like other successful provincial papers, it prints enough separate editions to cater to local interests. These kinds of papers generally contain few items of foreign news and they adopt a neutral line on domestic issues to avoid offending any of their readers.

Hard news reporting has never been one of the strong points of the French press on any level. French journalism has traditionally been a literary genre, strong on comment and embroidery and weak on facts; there is no real tradition of investigative reporting. This lack has been partly corrected in recent years by the success of the weekly news magazines. The three main rivals — *L'Express* and *Le Point* on the right and the socialist *Nouvel Observateur* — provide the public with weekly digests of current events, and they also have a full arts coverage. These three magazines are supplemented by the unique *Le Canard Enchaîné — The Enchained Duck —* a publication whose clever mixture of inside information, elegant mudslinging, irony and detachment makes it one of the world's most successful satirical journals.

France's record in the live arts over the postwar decades has been marked by great successes with performance works and in the diffusion of culture, but there has been an apparent falling-off in the level of individual creative achievement. In painting, for example, the days when France was able to take pride of place have passed. It is hard to think of any painters of the present generation who could rival such masters of the early 20th century as Henri Matisse or Georges Braque. New York has now taken over from Paris as the city where new art movements are born. The art market too is now centered on London and New York. Paris remains, though, a world capital for the display of works of art; its great museums, and in more recent years the large-scale temporary exhibitions that are organized at the Grand Palais and the Beaubourg Center, are in the foreground of international attention.

A happier picture is presented by the movies, a field in which France has excelled for a long time. A production studio existed in Paris as long ago as 1900, and a high proportion of the great names of film history, among them Jean Renoir, Marcel Carné and René Clair, have been French.

Fresh impetus was provided in the late 1950s with the arrival of the *nouvelle vague* — a new wave of young directors who were to transfigure the industry. Men and women such as François Truffaut, Agnès Varda and Jean-Luc Godard did not really belong to a single artistic school; but they shared an independence of mind that made them leery of corporate studio productions and eager to work within the constrictions of low budgets. They also shared the idea of the *film d'auteur* — the film as a personal creation, as much as a painting or a poem. The enthusiasm they injected into film making has carried the country's movie industry through many difficult times, and allowed it to expand when its rivals in most other countries have cut back drastically.

Today, France produces around 250 films each year, almost all of them on small budgets and many of them quirkily individual and difficult to classify. Few productions actually make much money, but costs are low enough not to scare away the investors. Such profusion has been possible because movie audiences have held up better in

France than in most European countries — largely because French television has provided such an unexciting alternative, cynics claim.

Attendances are far from uniform all over the country. In the provinces, there has been the same sorry tale of declining ticket sales and closing movie houses that has afflicted other nations. In Paris, though, movie houses and audiences have both increased: There are about 400 houses, most of them thriving. And since many of the movie houses are independently owned, there is no monopoly over the outlets for a film maker's work. In addition, there are thousands of film clubs all over France, often attached to schools or universities, which have done a great deal to educate new generations of viewers in the classics of the screen.

The theater in France in the past decade or two has been characterized by an absence of significant new playwrights and the emergence of a group of talented directors who have been introducing entirely new concepts of theater. Such innovators as Patrice Chéreau, Antoine Vitez and Ariane Mnouchkine show little respect for the written texts and instead their aim is to dazzle the spectator with the brilliance of their stage effects and the novelty of their interpretation — an approach to drama that is not always to everyone's taste but that can, at its best, produce startling results.

The most successful theaters have been not the old boulevard houses where attendances have been falling but the subsidized national companies. The venerable Comédie Française, founded by Louis XIV in 1680, concentrates mainly on the classics, which are performed in a traditional manner. The Théâtre National Populaire (TNP) was based for 42 years from its foundation in 1930 in Paris' Palais de Chaillot, where its name became synonymous with those of the great actor-director Jean Vilar and the male lead, Gérard Philipe. In 1972, however, the theater's name and subsidy were transferred to Roger Planchon's celebrated troupe in the Lyon suburb of Villeurbanne. In its old home in Paris, the Théâtre National de Chaillot was established in its stead; it is now under the direction of Antoine Vitez.

The transferal of the TNP was one of

A hundred and thirty feet above the square, visitors to the Beaubourg Center enjoy the view over Paris.

SIDESHOWS IN THE STREETS

When the Centre National d'Art et de Culture — also known as the Beaubourg Center from the square in which it stands, and as the Pompidou Center from the President who conceived and championed it — opened its doors to the public in 1977, it was expected to revitalize the decaying quarter bordering Les Halles where it is located. But few people could have foreseen the immediate influx of performers who have turned its plaza into France's main showcase for street theater. A constantly changing array of actors, mimes, dancers, fire-eaters, poets and musicians join with pavement artists and portraitists to entertain the 20,000 or so daily visitors, calling to mind the jugglers, acrobats and bear-baiters who in the Middle Ages performed a similar role outside another Paris landmark, Notre Dame Cathedral.

A dancer bends limbo-like backward toward the cobblestones.

A portraitist offers her wares from a pavement stall.

153

7

the most dramatic highlights of another trend noticeable in postwar French theater: the reawakening of the provinces, which, before 1945, showed few signs of cultural life. While in 1939 there were only a handful of permanent resident companies outside Paris, today there are more than 30, supported partly by the state and partly by the municipalities as well as by their own ticket sales. A similar tendency has been even more marked in the world of music, where something of a grass-roots revolution has taken place since the 1960s. There has been a full-scale revival of provincial opera, with a dozen or so permanent companies now scattered across the map of France. Audiences for orchestral and chamber music have also swelled vastly, as the younger generation has shown a growing interest in classical music. Nor are their activities confined to listening: The number of amateur choirs and consorts has also multiplied, and enrollments at music schools mushroomed from 250,000 in 1960 to over a million 20 years later.

This renewal of interest has in turn stimulated the Paris music scene. The national opera company in the Palais Garnier had a new lease on life in the 1970s under a German director, Rolf Liebermann, who restored it to the forefront of European companies. In addition, a modern opera house with expanded facilities is now under construction near the Bastille. And in 1972, President Pompidou personally persuaded France's greatest musical talent, Pierre Boulez, to return to his homeland after years of exile working in Germany, London and New York; the president's lure was the promise of an ambitious research center for modern music, now part of the arts complex

in the Beaubourg center. As a result, Paris, which was until recently backward in the performance of experimental music, is now a leading center of the European avant-garde.

Some of the credit for the spread of cultural activity to the regions can be attributed to government policy. In the 1960s, André Malraux, as Minister of Culture, had the grandiose idea of constructing multipurpose arts centers, to be known as Maisons de la Culture (Houses of Culture), in France's leading provincial cities, the costs to be shared between state and municipality. In practice, the policy had only limited success. Of the 60 or more establishments originally envisaged, only 15 were built, and in many cases they proved too large and expensive for local needs. In recent years, the program has been halted; in its place, towns have been encouraged to set up smaller "cul-

tural animation centers," which have proved financially more realistic and successful in attracting an audience unused to the theater or concert hall. The level of interest remains high, and many town councils take pride in devoting large sums of money to the arts, which are seen as a status symbol as well as a contribution to a district's quality of life.

Other, temporary venues for the performing arts are provided by the rash of festivals that have been established throughout France since the war. They are of many kinds. A majority, but by no means all, are in southern France, where the music festival at Aix-en-Provence and the theater festival at Avignon have both established themselves in the European front rank. Some festivals concentrate on the classics, others on modern works, and a few are folk-oriented, related to the revival of interest in regional traditions. Many a lovely old château is now the setting for some small gathering in summer, even if its program amounts to no more than a series of chamber concerts on Saturday evenings. At the other end of the scale are such large events as the music festival at Besançon, the Festival Estival or summer festival in Paris, that of theater and opera at Orange in Provence, and the general arts celebrations at La Rochelle on the Atlantic coast. However, rising costs have threatened some of the larger ventures, and organizers have been obliged to cut back on their scope.

The rise of culture in the provinces is one aspect of a much larger phenomenon in France today, the trend toward decentralization. The era of growth at any cost is dead, killed off as much by a revulsion from the more inhuman of its legacies — high-rise apartments, crowded highways — as by the economic slowdown of the 1970s. In its place there has been a return to local roots that has seen some of the centers of power moved out of the capital, Paris, and back to the provinces — a movement that runs completely counter to the general, centralizing tendency of French history.

Parallel to this provincial revival has been a new mood among the French in their approach to their expectations from life. Sociologists have christened it a *repli sur soi* — a turning in on oneself. The term, which implies a reliance on one's own inner strengths and resources rather than the outer-directed political and social concerns of the 1960s, has echoes in journalist Tom Wolfe's phrase for the America of the 1970s, "the me decade." But in France the mood has been less aggressive and

Signs advertising a local art exhibition adorn a housefront in a village in the Berry region of central France. The postwar cultural revival in the provinces runs the gamut from neighborhood displays of crafts to large-scale events such as the annual Avignon drama festival.

perhaps also less experimental, more concerned with rediscovering qualities of traditional life lost in the hectic modernism of the postwar years.

The picture, then, of France in the postwar years is one of a country old in its traditions coming face to face abruptly with the new. Twenty-five years of unparalleled economic growth radically altered its traditional way of life — perhaps too radically for the country to be able to come to terms with change. Coincidentally, economic progress has been slowed down first by the oil crises of the 1970s and then by the world recession of the early 1980s, leaving the nation time to ponder new solutions. Paradoxically, many French people have grown convinced that the way to find the right path forward is to look backward, so as to combine the best elements of the old France with the conveniences of the new. □

ACKNOWLEDGMENTS

The index for this book was prepared by Vicki Robinson. For their help with this volume, the editors also wish to thank: Jeanne Beausoleil, Curator, Collection Albert Kahn, Boulogne; Markie Benet, London; Suzanne Bicknell, London; Mike Brown, London; Marie Brunetto, Collobrières; Flavie Chaillet, Press Attaché, Hermès, Paris; Jeannette Chalufour, Archives Tallandier, Paris; Windsor Chorlton, London; Louise Earwaker, London; Michel Fleury, Paris; The French Embassy, London; The Library Staff of the French Institute, London; The French Government Tourist Office, London; Jeanne and Robert Halley, Caen, France; Liz Hodgson, London; Josiane Husson, Fédération Française du Prêt-à-Porter Féminin, Paris; Charles Jules-Rosette, Officer de Paix Principal, Paris; Sybille de Laforcade, Press Attaché, Chanel, Paris; Roy and Jenny Malkin, Andelot-en-Montagne, France; Claude Moinet, Grenoble; Christopher McIntosh, London; Claude Pianet, Press Attaché, Cartier, Paris; Baron Jacques de Sacy, Paris; Michèle Tapponier, Press Attaché, Fauchon, Paris; Deborah Thompson, London; Josseline Thille, Paris; Pascal de la Vaissière, Curator, Musée Carnavalet, Paris.

BIBLIOGRAPHY

BOOKS

Ardagh, John:
France in the 1980s. Penguin Books, Middlesex, 1982.
The New French Revolution. Secker and Warburg, London, 1968.
Rural France. Century Books, London, 1983.
Beaujeu-Garnier, J., *France,* in the series *The World's Landscapes.* Longman Group Ltd., London, 1975.
Brogan, D. W., and the Editors of Life, *France.* Life World Library, Time-Life Books, New York, 1960.
Bullough, Donald, *The Age of Charlemagne.* Elek Books, London, 1973.
Bury, J.P.T., *France 1814-1940.* Methuen and Co. Ltd., Revised ed. 1969.
Caron, François, *An Economic History of Modern France.* Methuen and Co. Ltd., London, 1979.
Charlton, F. G., ed., *France. A Companion to French Studies.* Methuen and Co. Ltd., London, 1979.
Chastel, André, *Paris.* Thames and Hudson, London, 1971.
Chelminski, Rudolph, *Paris.* The Great Cities, Time-Life Books, Amsterdam, 1977.
Cobban, Alfred, *A History of Modern France.* Penguin Books, Middlesex, 1965.
Debray, Régis, *Teachers, Writers, Celebrities, The Intellectuals of Modern France.* NLB, London, 1981.
Duby, Georges, and Robert Mandrou, *A History of French Civilisation.* Weidenfeld and Nicholson, London, 1964.
Dupeux, Georges, *French Society 1789-1970.* Methuen and Co. Ltd., London, 1976.
Feifer, Maxine, *Everyman's France.* J. M. Dent and Sons Ltd., London, 1982.
Frears, J. R., *France in the Giscard Presidency.* George Allen and Unwin, London, 1981.
Freiberg, J. W., *The French Press, Class, State and Ideology.* Praeger Publishers, New York, 1981.
Frémy, Dominique and Michèle, *Quid.* Robert Laffont, Paris, 1983.
Gramont, Sanche de, *The French, Portrait of a People.* Hodder and Stoughton, London, 1969.
Grunfeld, Frederic C., *The French Kings.* Time-Life Books, Amsterdam, 1983.
Guicharnaud, Jacques and June, *Modern French Theatre.* Yale University Press, New Haven and London, 1967.
Hanley, D. L., A. P. Kerr, and N. H. Waites, *Contemporary France, Politics and Society Since 1945.* Routledge and Kegan Paul Ltd., London, 1979.
Hibbert, Christopher, *The French Revolution.* Allen Lane, London, 1980.

Institut National de la Statistique et des Études Économiques, *Tableaux de l'Économie Française 1982. Annuaire Statistique de la France* 1981.
Jackson, J. Hampden, ed., *A Short History of France from Early Times to 1958.* University Press, Cambridge, 1959.
Jennett, Sean, *Paris.* B. T. Batsford Ltd., London, 1973.
Johnson, Douglas, *France.* Thames and Hudson, London, 1969.
Johnson, R. W., *The Long March of the French Left.* Macmillan, London, 1981.
Law, Joy, *Fleur de Lys, the Kings and Queens of France.* Hamish Hamilton, London, 1976.
Marnham, Patrick, *Lourdes.* William Heinemann Ltd., London, 1980.
Maurois, André, *From Proust to Camus, Profiles of Modern French Writers.* Weidenfeld and Nicolson, London, 1967.
Michaud, Guy, and Georges Torres, *Le Nouveau Guide France.* Hachette, Paris, 1982.
Michelin Green Guide Series, Michelin, Paris.
Mitford, Nancy, *The Sun King.* Harper and Row, New York, 1966.
Moody, Joseph N., *French Education since Napoleon.* Syracuse University Press, Syracuse, New York, 1978.
Nourissier, François, *The French.* Hutchinson and Co. Ltd., London, 1971.
Ouston, Philip, *France in the Twentieth Century.* Macmillan, London, 1972.
Peyrefitte, Alain, *The Trouble with France.* Alfred A. Knopf Inc., New York, 1981.
Pickles, Dorothy, *The Fifth French Republic.* Methuen and Co. Ltd., London, 1965.
Reid, Joyce M. H., *The Concise Oxford Dictionary of French Literature.* Clarendon Press, Oxford, 1976.
Rossiter, Stuart (editor), *Paris.* Blue Guides, Benn, London, 1968.
Serant, Paul, *La France des Minorités.* Robert Laffont, Paris, 1965.
Servan-Schreiber, Jean-Jacques, *The American Challenge.* Hamish Hamilton, London, 1968.
Seward, Desmond, *The Bourbon Kings of France.* Constable, London, 1976.
Thomson, David, *Democracy in France.* Oxford University Press, London, 1969.
Vaughan, Michalina, Martin Kolinsky, and Peta Sheriff, *Social Change in France.* Martin Robertson and Co. Ltd., Oxford, 1980.
Wallace-Hadrill, J. M., and John McManners, *France: Government and Society.* Methuen and Co. Ltd., London, 1970.
Werth, Alexander, *De Gaulle.* Penguin Books, Middlesex, England, 1965.

Willan, Anne, *French Regional Cooking.* Hutchinson, London, 1981.
Wylie, Laurence, *Village in the Vaucluse.* Harrap, London, 1961.
Young, Edward, ed., *The Shell Guide to France.* Michael Joseph, London, 1979.
Zeldin, Theodore, *France 1848-1945.* Oxford University Press, 1973-77.

PERIODICALS

Ball, Robert, "France's Risky Protectionist Fling," *Fortune International,* March 1983.
Financial Times Surveys:
"France," July 7, 1982.
"France: Banking, Finance and Investment," November 12, 1982.
Frears, J. R., "The Decentralisation Reforms in France," *Parliamentary Affairs,* Winter, 1983.
Kuhn, Raymond, "Broadcasting and Politics in France," *Parliamentary Affairs,* Winter, 1983.
Walker, Martin, "Mitterrand trapped in the Mays of History," *The Guardian,* May 12, 1983.

INDEX

Time-Life Books Inc. offers a wide range of fine recordings, including a *Big Bands* series. For subscription information, call 1-800-621-7026, or write TIME-LIFE MUSIC, Time & Life Building, Chicago, Illinois 60611.

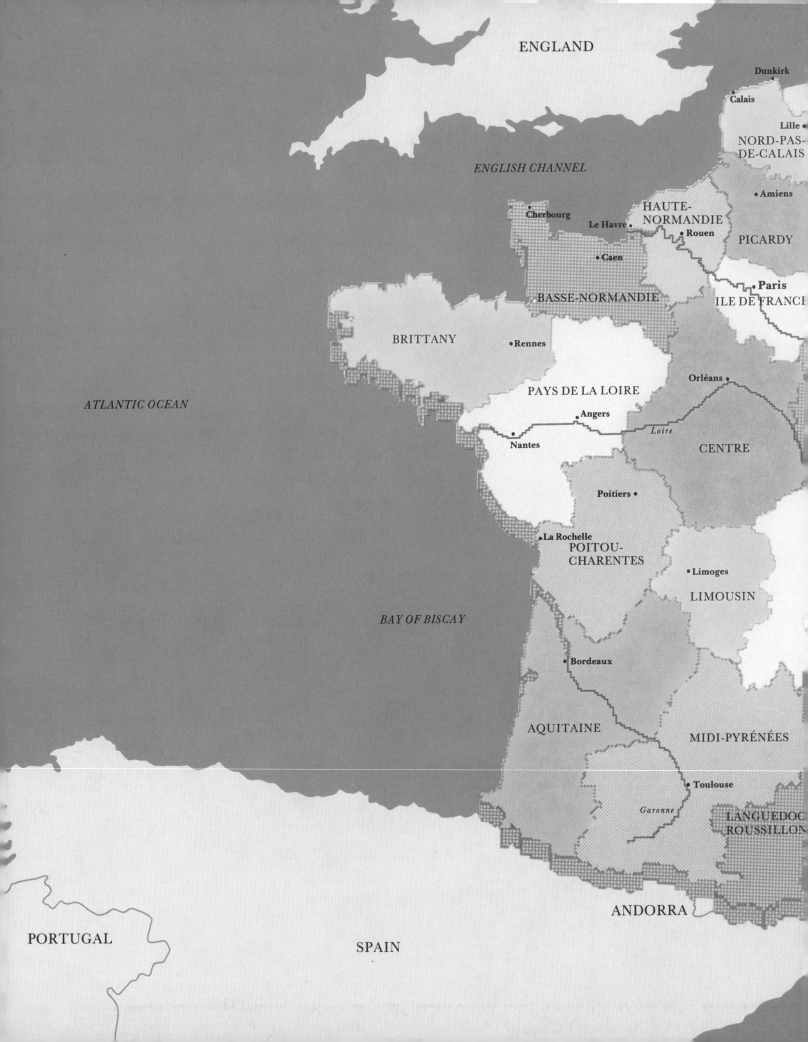